Edwin Gooch

Edwin Gooch

Champion of the Farmworkers

Simon Gooch

POPPYLAND
PUBLISHING

This edition 2020 published by Poppyland Publishing, Lowestoft, NR32 3BB.

www.poppyland.co.uk

ISBN 978 1 909796 73 7

Designed and typeset in 10.5 on 13.5 pt Gilamesh Pro.

Printed by Ashford Colour Press.

Picture credits:

All images are from the author's collection with the exception of pages 2, 85 (bottom), 101, which are courtesy of Gressenhall Museum of Norfolk Life.

It must never be forgotten that the lot of the agricultural worker is part and parcel of the lot of agriculture.

H. Rider Haggard, A Farmer's Year, 1899

Contents

"Old Boy" in a Norfolk jacket—a large format photograph from an Edwin Gooch album. He is possibly a relative.

The Old Boys

THE "old boys" used to be a familiar sight in the Norfolk and Suffolk countryside of my youth, seated by the fire in village pubs or leaning on a five-bar gate. They gathered weekly at the cattle market in Norwich that was then held in the protective shadow of the castle. Wearing flat caps, corduroys and old mackintoshes, sharing a well-aged joke, philosophising and politicking with strongly-held opinions—they were more or less as described in the accounts of farming life before the war by Adrian Bell, or recorded *verbatim* in the post-war oral histories of George Ewart Evans or Ronald Blythe. The old boys were the once indispensable but often overlooked agricultural workers, who had slowly decreased in numbers through a century of mechanisation.

When I first met them as a teenager our family was living just over the River Waveney in north Suffolk, having moved out of Norwich. In the late 1960s and 1970s these jovial and loquacious "old boys" were probably only in their middle-age, or perhaps just retired, but looking back now they seem figures from another time. Our nearest neighbour, across a field from which all the boundary hedges had recently been removed, was a remarkable character. A ploughman who had been interviewed by George Ewart Evans for his 1970 book *Where Beards Wag All*, he was full of dry East Anglian humour, tales of farming life and his one great adventure—serving overseas in the Great War.

Over many generations agricultural workers emerge very occasionally onto the national stage, in the Peasant's Revolt, Kett's Rebellion, the Swing Riots and the transportation of the Tolpuddle Martyrs. Times got so bad that they were forced to act. Otherwise they were the hired men of landowners or tenant farmers, "farm servants" limited in their role by a post-medieval class divide created by the dissolution of the monasteries and enclosures of common land. Unlike the peasantry of continental Europe they became, in a sense, strangers in their own land—though retaining their own rich culture.

In the 21st century, like the shire horses they once guided in front of the plough and lovingly tended, the old boys that I drank with in pubs that have long since closed down all seem to have disappeared. In an agriculture of big farms, vast machines, technicians and contractors, farmworkers have become solitary figures.

But there was once a halcyon time, within living memory, when they had at last received a fair deal thanks largely to their wartime efforts—their "place in the sun". Instead of insecurity of tenure and seasonal drops in earnings, after the Labour Party's election victory in 1945 agricultural workers achieved guaranteed minimum wages, regular hours and paid holidays—and could no longer be seen as anachronisms in the modern world.

This book is about the attempted resolution of those ancient inequities in the mid-20th century, told through the life of my grandfather Edwin Gooch, who played a leading part in that struggle for many years as the President of the National Union of Agricultural Workers (NUAW). He was also Labour MP for North Norfolk, first elected in the 1945 landslide. This history was conceived as his biography, but in the process of telling his story it has also become a tribute to all those "old boys" whose hopes for a better life in the countryside Edwin Gooch devoted so much of his time to achieving.

Simon Gooch 2020.

The Norfolk county banner, prominent at all NUAW demonstrations, required two men to carry it and four more on guy ropes.

The Spirit of Sweet Reasonableness

WHEN Edwin Gooch died in 1964 he was a household name in his native Norfolk, and well-known in Britain for his public roles in the National Union of Agricultural Workers and the Labour Party. He had devoted most of his life to politics and public administration, not in the sense of a conventional career (he was journalist and sub-editor on the *Norwich Mercury* until elected to Parliament) but as a calling, always on an honorary basis, acting from an ingrained dedication to the betterment of his fellow-citizens.

His home town of Wymondham—where he had lived all his life—came to a halt on the day of the funeral, shops closed in respect, farmworkers gathered in their Sunday suits. It was as if the old rural world was saying farewell to one who had helped bring it into modern society, working to banish the old inequalities and habits of deference. Though national figures were in attendance, this was essentially a local event, with the sturdy and phlegmatic East Anglian character that Edwin himself personified in both manner and voice. He was proud to be a "son of Norfolk".

Edwin Gooch followed on directly from the pioneers of rural radicalism in the county, in particular the legendary George Edwards who chose him as his honorary agent in 1918 and then promoted him as his successor in the trade union and the Labour Party in South Norfolk. By his dedication to the farmworkers' cause, Edwin helped at last—after the desperate battles for recognition in the 1920s, the universal hard times of the 1930s and the collective war effort—to bring stability and respect to an often precarious area of employment.

In his lifetime he saw a great transformation in farming methods. The consequent reduction in the workforce was the undertow that sapped much of the strength of agricultural trade unionism in more recent times and weakened the identity of rural communities, and yet created a new emphasis on technical skills for the younger generation employed on farms. The inevitability of change would eventually force the NUAW, described by Edwin in the 1940s as "one of the wonders of the trade union world", to merge with the mighty Transport & General Workers Union, now Unite, twenty years after he died.

This pragmatic decision did not stop the old forces of political reaction and the new giants of agri-business threatening to undermine rural labour—as shown by the controversial abolition of the Agricultural Wages Board in England (established in its supposedly permanent form by Labour's 1947 legislation) by the Coalition Government in 2013. Uncertainty remains a fact of a life for the farmworker, though in practice a good farmer will always value a good worker.

Edwin Gooch carried the spirit of George Edwards' belief in the power of "sweet reasonableness" throughout his time in the Union and in Parliament. However, this ideal could never be taken for granted, and when his preferred co-operation with the farmers was compromised or undermined by bad faith, he would not hesitate to call out the miscreants in public.

I was nine-years-old when he died, and my strongest memories of him are of a pipe-smoking 'Grandpa', routinely offering me aromatic "baccy" from his pouch when we went to call on a weekend "down Wymondham", and of an old man basking in the garden. But even as a child I could sense reserves of strength, and something beyond the average in his personal significance. I was a little shy of him as a result, though he was a kindly man with a very Norfolk sense of humour and his manner was always cheery. I can still recall his equable response of "fair to middling" whenever asked how he was, and his rather period farewells: "Toodle-pip!" or "Toodle-oo!".

We once went to visit him in the House of Commons, the family sitting together in easy chairs in the Members' Tea Room, and my only regret is that I never heard that broad Norfolk accent in the chamber itself when speaking on behalf of his farmworker brothers in the righteous but never solemn manner of George Edwards and Joseph Arch before him.

Edwin's second wife and widow Mollie suggested I might write a biography one day, and I have toyed with the idea in the twenty years since she died. I carried out relevant researches for a family history some while ago, and it was a particular pleasure to read back numbers of the Land Worker and thereby get a very vivid idea of the world in which Edwin Gooch operated. In the 1930s the journal might promote Soviet collectivisation, but always used a romantic woodcut of a country scene on its front cover. Those researches at Transport House, courtesy of the then editor of Landworker Mike Pentelow, and at the University of Reading's NUAW Archive, form the backbone of this biography.

I have since inherited photograph albums that are a happy confusion of family gatherings, holidays on the beach at Wells or on the Broads, and political conferences—an evocative visual compensation for the lack of personal papers: Edwin died in office, and had no time and probably no inclination to write a memoir.

A series of substantial academic works on agricultural trade unionism in the 20th century have had quite a bit to say about Edwin Gooch—sometimes critical from an ideological standpoint, as is the way with most political history, but always acknowledging his integrity and achievement. One question posed by these studies remains unanswerable: could a more radical approach have achieved more lasting benefits for the farmworkers?

The recent inclusion of Edwin Gooch in the *Dictionary of National Biography*, with an entry written by the late Professor Alun Howkins of the University of Sussex, made me finally sit up and think that there might be a case for a book that showed in more detail and individual character how in so many marches, committees, articles and speeches (whether on a conference platform or on top of an old hay wain on a village green) Edwin Gooch dedicated his life to the good old cause of improving the lot of the working man in the countryside.

The Land Worker has a long and distinguished history of fine illustrated front covers.

The family forge on Fairland Street, Wymondham, c1905 — "S.Gooch & Son. Shoeing smiths. Wholesale fork & shoe makers". Edwin Gooch is standing by the door, next to his brother Albert and father Simon.

Forge and Chapel

EDWIN Gooch's known forebears were living in villages in South Norfolk from the early 18th century, where even now the surname is relatively common. James Gooch was a yeoman farmer of Seething who married Ann Brabant—presumably from a "Stranger" family, Protestant refugees from the Spanish Netherlands—at Ditchingham in 1722. Their third son William was a blacksmith at Woodton (the old forge still stands by the main Norwich to Bungay road), and by his Will of 1779 he bequeathed his "stock of Working Tools commonly used in the trade of blacksmith" to his eldest son James. Edwin was descended from James and his fourth wife Sarah Harvey, and then their second son John Gooch, a blacksmith and veterinary surgeon.

Edwin's father Simon Gooch was born in Woodton in 1842, the fourth son of John and Elizabeth. His eldest brother Henry took over the family forge, so Simon had to look for work elsewhere. When Simon Gooch married Ellen Stackard in 1864 at Kirstead, he described himself like his father as a veterinary surgeon—a rural healing role that traditionally went with that of blacksmith or farrier.

Edwin Gooch's formidable and influential mother Ellen, née Stackard.

Their first child, Laura Matilda, was born in Wymondham in 1865, but died the next year in Birmingham, where the Goochs briefly lived. Simon's brother-in-law Stephen Stackard (or Stackyard) had already set himself up in business in the booming Midland city as a manufacturer of wine merchants' requisites, and he and his son Stephen would do well for themselves in that line and later in glass bottle manufacture.

Simon Gooch was described as a brewer's agent when his baby daughter died, but this venture came to nothing. Simon and Ellen Gooch soon returned to Norfolk, where their first son, Frederick, was born in 1868, back in Kirstead.

At the 1871 Census they were established again in Wymondham; Simon was a blacksmith, living in Damgate Street and working for Thomas Hubbard. Ellen was a dressmaker, and they had two children, Fred and Lilian. In about 1876, according to his obituary, "he commenced in business for himself as a smith and machinist etc". 'S. Gooch' was listed in Kelly's Norfolk Directory for 1879 as a farrier, working on his own account at 16 Fairland Street, Wymondham, where the house and workshop they occupied for the next thirty or more years can still be seen. (The old forge was used as such by a decorative metalworker until relatively recently.)

Michael Gooch, son of Edwin and Ethel, visiting the old forge in Wymondham, 1996.

The Gooch family expanded in the usual Victorian way, ultimately to ten children, three of whom had died by the time of the 1911 Census. Edwin George Gooch was the youngest, born on 15th January 1889—perhaps something of an afterthought, as his next sibling Ethel was five years older than him. His eldest sister Lily, about nineteen when he was born, was in some ways a second mother to Edwin and they remained close in later life. A photograph shows the infant Edwin Gooch with a small girl who is his niece "Moss", daughter of Lily, who had married Percy Reyner and gone to live in London.

In 1881 Simon Gooch had his son Frederick, 14, as a blacksmith's apprentice, and employed one man who lodged with the family at Fairland Street. Ten years later Frederick had moved on to join the police force and his brother Albert V, 15, was helping his father. In 1901 a 13-year-old boy from Brooke was working at the forge with Simon, replacing Albert who had set up on his own with a smithy at Hingham. In 1911 Simon Gooch, aged 67, was a master blacksmith.

The doughty Simon Gooch, as a Primitive Methodist, a member of various Friendly Societies and a Liberal, undoubtedly influenced his son Edwin in his religious, social and political views. Edwin later paid tribute to the moral influence of his mother, too. Their rather formidable blend of nonconformist high-mindedness, political radicalism and personal discipline (in their adherence to teetotalism) derived from a very particular Norfolk strain of independence of mind. Another Wymondham radical, Robert Kett, had led a celebrated armed revolt in the 16th century—and Simon Gooch is said to have forged the steel bands

Edwin Gooch, born 1889, and his niece Jessie "Moss" Reyner, born 1894, daughter of his eldest sister Lily, born 1870.

that still keep Kett's Oak, on the old main road to Norwich, from collapse— but Victorian and Edwardian nonconformists who tended towards Socialism preferred a peaceable resistance to oppression. Adherence to Christian principle was fundamental; the Bible was their text, not *Das Kapital*.

The Methodist tradition of the lay preacher was strong in the county, and produced pioneer trade unionists—confident public speakers, of whom George Edwards remains the paramount example. For most of the 19th century the political party for nonconformists was the Liberals. In 1891 "S. Gooch" was listed in a report by the *Norwich Mercury* on a meeting of the National Agricultural Labourers Union at Wymondham where Joseph Arch, the first leader of a farmworkers' trade union and a Liberal MP, urged the crowd to vote for the "Grand Old Man", William Ewart Gladstone.

The Primitive Methodist Connexion was a radical evangelical movement that split with "respectable" Wesleyanism in 1811 and did not reunite with them until 1932. To detractors they were "The Ranters". There are Gooch family photos of Wymondham Primitive Methodist gatherings—sports and festivities mostly, in the recreation ground behind the chapel—illustrating the denomination's active social role. Both Arch and Edwards were "Prims".

This devotion to Christian principle gave great impetus to Socialism in the

"Muscular Methodists" making a recreation ground behind the Wymondham chapel. Edwin Gooch stands centrally with wide-brim hat and spade; his future father-in-law Charles Dawson Banham is next but one to his left; Sarah Banham stands at far left.

countryside, inspiring men to escape the strictures of Tory squire and parson. (Two of the Tolpuddle Martyrs had been Wesleyan lay preachers.) Union meetings in the late 19th century were often held in chapels or at open-air camp meetings, where men could speak freely.

Only two photographs survive of Simon Gooch. One shows him and his formidable wife Ellen, circa 1910, in their Sunday best, out on a country walk with their very dapper son Edwin (who is wearing a bowler hat and a fancy waistcoat), his future wife Ethel Banham, and grandson Bill. Another is of the exterior of the family forge; Simon is in his smith's leather apron, with three assistant farriers, including a young Edwin—the photo was probably taken shortly after he left school in about 1905. The sign above the door reads "Simon Gooch & Co, Shoeing Smiths, Wholesale Fork Manufacturers". A surviving bill, dated 1904, is headed "S. Gooch & Son, Shoeing Smiths, Machinists & Agricultural Engineers, Repairers of Harvesting & Barn Machines, Ploughs, Harrows, Grass Cutters, Hurdles &c. Wholesale Makers of Hay & Harvest Forks, Rakes & Hoes".

A 1912 obituary for Simon Gooch in the local press, probably written by Edwin and headed 'Popular Tribute to an Old Tradesman', noted admiringly that "Throughout the years he has been at his wonted place at the forge, rarely missing a day through illness. Within a fortnight of his death he was engaged in his business as usual to the accompaniment of the ring of his hammer on the anvil". He had "served on a town committee or two" and was "a fireman in the days of the old hand engine". As well as an ardent Liberal, he was a Past Grand

Edwin Gooch and his fiancee Ethel Banham out on a Sunday stroll with his parents Simon and Ellen and their grandson Bill.

Master of the local Loyal Agincourt lodge of the Oddfellows and a member of two teetotal friendly societies—the Independent Order of Rechabites and the Good Templar Order (whose splendid banner is in the Wymondham Heritage Museum). Simon had once represented the Norfolk District Lodge at the Annual Sessions of the Good Templar Grand Lodge of England in London.

At the cemetery, the Rev Percy Jackson of the Primitive Methodist Church described Simon Gooch's self-deprecatory, upright nature:

> We are here today mourning the loss of an honest man. In one way one cannot but admire that candour with himself which hindered his definitely joining the Church. Recognising the high demands of Christian discipleship, he shrank back from formal adherence to the ranks of the Church. And that as he thought for the Church's sake. But he was nevertheless a follower of Jesus, staunch in the integrity of his soul, fearless of all consequences of right doing, a hater of shame and crookedness, an ardent lover of fair play and justice. God loveth such to worship Him. This man was well used to humble himself before the presence of God. His devoutness in worship, and his eager attentiveness to that expounded word, were an example to a congregation, and many a time has the Christian preacher been encouraged by this rapt devotion,

and Simon Gooch's 'Amen' at the end of a sermon was something to send a preacher to his next task with joy in his heart.

These tributes to Simon Gooch and his steadfast character have a familiar ring—those directed to his son Edwin over fifty years later were of a similar, if more secular, nature.

Ellen Gooch at the door of the family home beside the forge in Fairland Street, Wymondham, probably after Simon Gooch's death in 1912.

Charles Dawson Banham, his wife Sarah and their children at The Gas House, Station Road, Wymondham, c1900. Ethel Banham standing left.

Edwin Gooch standing behind his fiancée Ethel at a Banham family gathering in Wymondham c1913.

Severe damage inflicted on the Norwich Mercury works when the Wensum flooded, 1912.

The Norwich Mercury

EDWIN Gooch was probably the first male member of his family to get a decent and fairly lengthy education. After the Central Boys' School on Browick Road in Wymondham, Edwin attended Duke Street Higher Grade School in Norwich, the precursor to the City of Norwich School. He would have travelled in every day by bus. Wymondham—very grand in many ways for a market town—would always remain his home, his political base and the source of great pride, but much of his life was spent in Norwich.

On leaving Duke Street, aged about sixteen, Edwin worked for a short while in the family forge, but soon left to become articled as a printer in the composing room of that old-established Liberal-supporting twice-weekly newspaper *The Norwich Mercury*. Perhaps there was a traditional link between school and paper, as the works were nearby, fronting the River Wensum.

Edwin rose rapidly from compositor to be a staff reporter on the *Mercury* by 1911 (when he was described at the Census, living with his parents in Fairland Street, as "Printer & Reporter"). From 1912 Edwin Gooch was a member of the National Union of Journalists (founded in 1907), and remained in the NUJ for the rest of his life, despite his much more significant role in the National Union of Agricultural Workers.

In August 1912 a terrible flood wrecked the *Norwich Mercury's* St George's Works amongst many other properties in the city and beyond, and several lives were lost. Edwin had been at the printing works when the lower section of its riverside end wall gave way. The presses subsequently moved to Redwell Street, on higher ground and closer to the picturesque old multi-gabled and jettied editorial offices of the *Mercury* at 45 London Street. A later press photo shows Edwin Gooch, wearing his best roving reporter outfit—a very natty homburg, overcoat and spats—in a

Newshound Edwin Gooch in a group accompanying King George V and the Bishop of Norwich as they inspect a river-widening scheme after the 1912 floods.

The journalists and printers of the Norwich Mercury in their charabancs outside a Norfolk pub on their annual outing or "wayzgoose".

A Norwich Mercury wayzgoose, before and after.

gaggle accompanying King George V and the Bishop of Norwich as they inspect progress on a river-widening scheme after the floods.

Other photographs, post-1918, show a carefree group of journalists and office boys off on a summertime spree or 'wayzgoose' (a word peculiar to the printing industry that may derive from letting geese out to glean for grain in the 'ways' between the stubble), an escape from the cacophony of the *Mercury's* presses. Such days out were spent rolling down Norfolk lanes in a couple of charabancs, heading for some bucolic public house. Of the party is the strict teetotaller Edwin Gooch. One group photo shows the men formed up in rows, looking serious; and another, taken seconds later after a wisecrack, shows them all in stitches.

Edwin Gooch and press cronies at the annual fair on Norwich Cattle Market.

Edwin was still travelling between Wymondham and Norwich, initially from Fairland Street in his bachelor days, and catching the last bus home after putting the paper to bed. Then not long after war broke out in 1914 his protracted courtship of Ethel Banham culminated in their marriage at Wymondham. The couple had already begun building a house in the town, with the help of a Co-operative Society mortgage. The Wordsworthian *Rydal Mount* stood at the junction of the Norwich Road and a narrow lane that would be renamed

Vimy Ridge post-war. The builder's final invoice from 1915 survives, for £324-17-11. The house was not large or luxurious, and was lit by gas until the arrival of electricity in the 1930s; mains water came about the same time—until then it was pumped from a well. The lavatory was an outdoor thunderbox, with the nightsoil collected once a week.

Judging by the many group photographs in old albums, the substantial back garden at *Rydal Mount* became the setting for most big family gatherings of the ramifying local tribe of Goochs, Banhams, Reyners, Lanes and Hayes in future years, including a Golden Wedding celebration for the Banham parents. (Very much later, one pleasant afternoon get-together almost ended in disaster when the present writer, aged about seven or eight, lost control of a lawnmower that was sent careering towards the then venerable subject of this biography until Edwin's son Michael intervened.)

Ethel Banham had been born in Wisbech in 1887, and her immediate family always spoke with a 'Fenny' accent or brogue. A few years later her father Charles Dawson Banham moved to Wymondham to manage the town's small gasworks on Station Road, which before the arrival of a by-pass in more modern times was a continuation of Fairland Street. Like the Goochs the Banhams were Primitive Methodists. A postcard made from a photo taken pre-1914 and labelled 'Muscular Methodists',

Edwin and Ethel Gooch outside their Wymondham home, 'Rydal Mount', with dog Laski.

Edwin and Ethel Gooch in the garden of Percy and Lily Reyner's house, Belsize Park, c1915

shows several members of both families (including Edwin Gooch and his future father-in-law Charles Dawson Banham) clearing an old orchard to make a sports ground behind the church at Town Green (see p.10).

Ethel was very well-educated for a working class woman of the period, having attended East Dereham High School. She went on to train as a schoolteacher at the women-only Homerton College, Cambridge, from 1906-9. While she was there her determined suitor Edwin Gooch visited, presumably by bicycle, or perhaps motorcycle, and sent a postcard to her c/o Homerton College on his safe return home announcing gratefully "no punctures". By the time that the photograph of the courting couple was taken pre-1914, together with Edwin's parents and nephew Bill on a Sunday afternoon stroll (p.11), Ethel was probably back in Wymondham after a spell at Great Hockham village school in the Brecklands, and would have been teaching at the town's Junior School. Though it was obligatory for a female teacher to leave the profession on marrying, the wartime manpower shortage meant that Ethel stayed on. She would rise to become headmistress.

From all the evidence the Banhams in general had intellectual, not to say pedagogical, strengths. Charles Dawson Banham's 1896 report on the problematical gasworks at Wells-next-the-Sea, that he had been asked to inspect by the Urban District Council, is a model of clarity, concision and common sense. Ethel's younger brother Percy or "Pip" Banham was to marry Edwin's niece Violet "Pat" Reyner in 1921, and their eldest son Peter Reyner Banham would become a celebrated architectural critic, writer and academic. His brother Paul was a teacher specialising in languages and natural history.

Edwin's much-loved mother, Ellen, died in 1917, and though not a lot is known about her she seems to have been as much a moral influence on him as her late husband Simon. The success of her brother Stephen in the bottle-making business suggests that the Stackards, despite their humble origins, were entrepreneurial by nature. The Stackard sons were educated at the Merchant Taylors School in the City of London. During the Great War Edwin's cousin Harold Stackard was an air ace in the Royal Naval Air Service, with fifteen 'victories' in Sopwith Pups and Camels. In contrast, a snapshot from 1917 shows Edwin nonchalantly smoking a cigarette in the uniform of the Volunteer Force, the Home Guard of its day. The volunteers were known colloquially as 'The Old and the Bold' and wore armbands with 'GR', signifying 'Georgius Rex'; they were inevitably also dubbed the 'Gorgeous Wrecks'.

The wider family suffered several losses in the war, including Edwin's brother-in-law Victor Hayes, killed at Passchendaele, and two of Ethel's brothers were in Mesopotamia with the Norfolk Regiment, so to have at least one male at home (presumably for medical reasons) must have been a relief for all concerned. After discharge in September 1919 Edwin received a certificate of service with the printed signature of Winston Churchill, Secretary of State for War, thanking Private Edwin George Gooch of the 4th Volunteer Battalion Norfolk Regiment on behalf of the King for his three years of service from November 1916.

'The Old and the Bold': Edwin Gooch as a Volunteer, 1917.

Immediately post-war, snapshots show off Edwin's Rudge motorcycle sidecar outfit, once driven down to London to visit his eldest sister Lily and her wood engraver husband Percy Reyner. Such jaunts presumably ended when a son, Michael Edwin Gooch, was born in 1923 at Wymondham. Having waited nine years for a child, Edwin and Ethel were indulgent parents, judging by the albums of miniscule Kodak snaps of him as a well-wrapped baby and as a toddler. Scores of photos of Michael and his young Banham cousins evoke a very congenial round of family socialising.

Like his father Michael would later travel into Norwich to go to school and remembered often visiting the

Edwin, Ethel and the Rudge motorcycle and sidecar.

Mercury as a boy, the great din and drama of hot metal typesetting and the mighty presses going full throttle. One of the linotype compositors gave him a strip of freshly-minted type forming his name. The then editor, George Rye, had only one arm—he'd lost the other in the war—and this, too, fascinated the young schoolboy.

Edwin's journalist's salary allowed them to own a sailing boat on the Broads— the *Nancy*—and a beach hut ('Leisure Hours') at Wells-next-the-Sea, which could be easily reached by train from Wymondham via Melton Constable. Many family photos feature boat or hut, or other seaside gatherings, with Edwin always fully clothed and usually wearing a hat, but *Nancy* was sold in the mid-Twenties for fear of the young Michael falling overboard; the beach hut was dismantled by the Army in 1940, in case the Germans decided to invade via Holkham Bay— official compensation was £70.

On board the 'Nancy'. Edwin and Ethel Gooch with baby Peter Reyner Banham, his mother Pat and grandfather Percy Reyner, Norfolk Broads 1922.

George Edwards, founder of the Union, speaking to farmworkers from a waggon, 1920s.

Mr Edwards with his Agent

IT was while working on the *Norwich Mercury* that Edwin Gooch first became involved in pioneer Labour Party organisation in the county. Norwich had long been a stronghold for trade unionism and socialism since William Morris spoke to great crowds in the market place in the 1880s, and a branch of the Independent Labour Party was first set up there in the 1890s. However, local constituency parties did not exist until the Labour Party Constitution was drawn up in 1918 by Sidney Webb, in the wake of the granting of limited suffrage to women and full suffrage to working class men.

For a time Edwin was chairman of the NUJ's Norfolk and Norwich Branch, then in October 1918 was appointed part-time constituency agent by the newly-established South Norfolk Divisional Labour Party in Wymondham. His elder brother Albert had been a founder member, and Edwin and Ethel soon joined him.

Edwin Gooch thus got to know and become a close ally and friend of the candidate for the South Norfolk seat, the veteran trade union pioneer George Edwards, a lovable figure who is remembered with great affection to this day, especially by farmworkers and especially in his home county. Edwards was formally adopted in November 1918, a week after the Armistice, and spoke of his hopes that the League of Nations would bring universal brotherhood. He argued for a just and permanent peace with no vindictiveness, perceiving (with great foresight) that Germany should not be crushed or she would prepare for another war, in comparison to which the past war would be as nothing. The press reported the proceedings, which concluded with George stating "He did not suppose he should live to see it, but he wanted the land nationalised. (Cheers)."

Hunched and lopsided after a hard life on the land, and a physical collapse just before the war broke out, Edwards was nevertheless a man capable of quite heroic endurance—a "tough old forest oak". He had been born in poverty at Marsham, in north Norfolk, in 1850. After suffering years of economic hardship, and having been thrown out of many farming jobs and tied cottages for his political activism, he had set up the Eastern Counties Agricultural Labourers' and Smallholders' Union in 1906 at North Walsham. He was thereby consciously taking up the baton from Joseph Arch's pioneer National Agricultural Labourers' Union, of which George had been a stalwart, but which had folded in the depressed 1890s.

George cycled all over the county, setting up branches and recruiting men in what was almost a one-man revival of agricultural trade unionism. He used his experience as a lay preacher to speak in a clear, forthright style, usually taking a Biblical text as his starting point, at large open air Sunday "camp meetings" that would begin with a prayer and end with a hymn.

Gladstone's 1884 Representation of the People Act had given the vote to male rural workers who paid over £10 per annum in rent or who owned property of at least that value. They rewarded the Liberal Party (for which they were often victimised by their Tory-supporting employers) but in the early years of the 20th century would begin to shift their allegiance to Labour. After a landslide victory in the 1906 General Election, the Liberals had delivered old age pensions, and passed the Small Holdings Act in 1909 but still came to be associated with the landowners rather than the land workers, despite the introduction of punitive death duties. In this supposed golden age of Edwardian plenty, the clarion call of Socialism was creating a militant atmosphere on the farms, particularly in Norfolk.

The turning point for the new Union was the 1910 farmworkers' strike at St Faith's, just outside Norwich, led by its branch secretary George Hewitt—a future President and General Secretary in its later incarnation as the National Union of Agricultural Workers. The strike was resolved at the behest of the Liberals, anxious that a general election was in the offing. This was very unpopular with the men and at the next annual conference in Fakenham in

Farmworkers giving three cheers for NUALRW President George Edwards.

February 1911 Hewitt, and local allies such as Bill Holmes and Walter Smith, got a motion passed condemning the "dishonourable" closing down of the strike, after which there had been considerable victimisation. In the ensuing upheaval Smith became President, though Edwards (who had been in the minority voting against ending the strike on the farmers' terms) remained General Secretary, but the new Executive became in effect Labour-supporting.

The renamed National Union of Agricultural Labourers and Rural Workers—its great county banner bearing the exclamatory exhortation "Agitate! Educate!! Organize!!!"—formally changed affiliation from Liberal to Labour in 1913, and began to expand nationwide from its Norfolk base. By the outbreak of war in 1914 the Union was making progress in its demand for a living wage; George Edwards had stepped down due to ill health, and a dynamic Scottish socialist, Robert Barrie Walker, became General Secretary. In a personal intervention Walker obtained much improved conditions on the Royal Estate at Sandringham, after deploying the inspired slogan "The King's Pay and the King's Conditions".

In parallel with efforts to improve wages and terms of employment, there was an attempt to create a true local democracy at the parish level. The Burston School Strike, near Diss in south Norfolk, was sparked by victimisation of the village schoolteacher Tom Higdon, a Labour Party and NUALRW Executive member. Higdon successfully removed the local cabal of vested interests—farmers, chiefly—from the parish council by the election of farmworkers in their stead.

As a result Tom and his wife Annie were sacked by Norfolk Education Committee in April 1914, at the instigation of Burston's inflexible and vindictive parish priest, but their pupils walked out in protest the same day. They were educated independently by the Higdons from then on. The Burston Strike School was opened in 1917 and remains a remarkable monument to a time of real and bitter confrontation in the countryside and to genuine working class solidarity; the facade is inscribed with donors' names, often of long-defunct trade unions and exotic individuals such as Count Leo Tolstoy, emigre son of the author. The Strike School only closed in

Scenes from the Longest Strike. Edwin's snapshots of the Burston Strike School, opened in 1917, and the annual rally c1920.

February 1940, a few months after Tom Higdon's death, when the remaining children were transferred to the Council School.

Wartime conditions and food crises changed everything in the status of the agricultural workers. The U-boat blockade came close to starving Britain of vital food supplies in 1916, until a convoy system was belatedly introduced for merchant shipping. Manpower shortages—about 400,000 farmworkers having either volunteered or been conscripted—inspired initiatives such as the Women's National Land Service Corps, but also took children aged as young as eleven out of school to work on the farms. Prisoners of war were, of course, a source of free labour. Wages went up for the remaining men, and with the Corn Production Act of 1917 not only were cereal prices guaranteed, but also Agricultural Wages Boards—at county and national level—were set up to establish minimum wages and maximum hours by negotiation (though county by county, rather than across the nation). In Norfolk the farmworkers' wages rose to 30/- for 54 hours in summer, 48 hours in winter, with overtime pay and a Saturday half-holiday.

Robert Walker, with his preference for a centralised organisation, as articulated through the newspaper *The Labourer*, moved the headquarters to London from Fakenham in 1918, and the Union was again renamed (this time more economically) the National Union of Agricultural Workers in 1920. In this new, apparently securely supported industry, Union membership soared. The NUAW had 170,000 men in 1919; the Workers Union, which for a time rivalled it in some areas—mainly in North-West England—had 100,000. The Scottish Farm Servants Union was also growing north of the border. George Edwards later marvelled at his Union's progress from a little back room in his cottage at Gresham to Headland House, its substantial premises on Gray's Inn Road, London.

Edwin Gooch, who was a younger man than all of the main Union figures at that time, would act as George Edwards's honorary agent in several Parliamentary elections, and was later thanked in George's autobiography for his valuable help undertaken "without promise of any fee or reward". In the first of these battles, the December 1918 'Khaki Election' called by Lloyd George in the brief moment of euphoria immediately after the Armistice, Edwards stood for Labour, losing South Norfolk to the Liberal Coalition candidate W.H.Cozens-Hardy. The electorate included women for the first time (though only those over the age of thirty, with a property qualification) and all working class men over the age of twenty-one (that is, the millions formerly excluded by property or rental restrictions), thereby changing the nature and scope of British politics for good.

Despite the greatly expanded franchise, Labour lost out to the patriotic mood of the nation. Nevertheless, after the South Norfolk poll, in a continuing spirit of wartime unity, the winning and losing candidates held a joint meeting in the Fairland Hall in Wymondham to celebrate what Edwards called "the cleanest and purest political fight that ever was fought... It was expressed by both sides that we had lifted the political life of South Norfolk on to a high level".

In a letter of thanks to his helpers George Edwards wrote: "My one hope is that you will go forth with renewed vigour, organise your forces, exercise patience and sweet reasonableness. I hope to live to see South Norfolk go solid for Labour."

Labour's top priority in the aftermath of this disappointment was to organise properly on a local basis—until 1918 the party had relied on union branches and socialist clubs—and in April 1919 the *Eastern Daily Press* announced "Lord Kimberley Opens Wymondham Labour Institute". A press photo shows the peer who, residing at nearby Kimberley Park, had been the first in the House of Lords to declare for Labour. He was highly regarded in Norfolk for paying his farmworkers more than the rate demanded by the NUAW. 'The Labour Earl', as the papers dubbed him, stands shoulder to shoulder with George Edwards, Edwin Gooch and others at the new premises in Church Street, opposite the Abbey.

Once the Earl unlocked the door and declared the Institute open, the *Eastern Daily Press* continued: "This formal ceremony was followed by a tea, generously given by Mrs E.G.Gooch, in which 100 participated." At a public meeting held there that evening the Earl of Kimberley "said that although they had only been in existence for twelve months, yet during that time they had been very precocious. They were suddenly called up to perform a herculean task, for they had tried to place his old friend Mr George Edwards on the top of the poll. Although he was beaten by a considerable majority, he was not down-hearted. He (the speaker) knew something about elections, having been in a number of them. Elections were not won by going about making speeches, they were won by office work. They had a good Labour Party in South Norfolk, and he would be disappointed if they did not return a Labour candidate at the next election. At the time of the last election they had hardly cut their first tooth. They had to try when there was another General Election to send Mr George Edwards to Parliament."

The chance would come sooner than he anticipated. In the meantime Labour agitation remained intense in 1919, a year of political crisis that verged on open revolt in 'Red Clydeside' and with battleships sent to curb unrest in Liverpool. Fear of a Bolshevik-style takeover gripped the Coalition Government and the press. The state of the countryside was not so tumultuous, but feelings were running high. The Museum of Norfolk Life at Gressenhall has an NUALRW poster from 1919 advertising a 'Great Demonstration' at the Fairland, Wymondham, with two trade unionists speaking on the revolutionary land nationalisation theme "Our Land and How to Get It": "Come in Your Thousands to Hear Labour's Orators". In the chair (a position he was to occupy on various bodies and committees, at home and abroad, for the next forty or more years) was E.G.Gooch, President, Wymondham Labour Party.

From January 1920 Edwin Gooch was Secretary *pro tem* to the South Norfolk Labour Party, and for several years the Minutes are in his handwriting; stuck into the opening page is a clipping ostensibly about the retirement of a local railwayman, with the resonant headline "Setting a Train on Its Way" (the National Union of Railwaymen having part-financed the purchase of the Labour Institute). By this time Edwin had been joined by his newly-enfranchised wife Ethel on the Executive Committee. With his brother Albert—now back in Wymondham running the forge in Fairland Street—a regular on the EC since 1918, that made three Goochs at the South Norfolk top table! Edwin's prominent role in local politics seems to have been opposed by the Primitive Methodists, and he apparently resigned as a lay preacher and a member of the congregation in 1920, while remaining in sympathy with the church's tenets.

In November 1919 George Edwards had declined to stand again for Parliament on medical grounds, having collapsed after a visit to Buckingham Palace to be appointed CBE. But in June 1920 a by-election was called when Cozens-Hardy inherited peerage. Edwin Gooch was proposed as candidate, but subsequently withdrew; instead W.B.Taylor was proposed by Ethel Gooch. He won a ballot of members, but the NUAW seemed to be unwilling or unable to finance his campaign. At a last-minute summit between Walter Smith MP, President of the Union, and the Divisional Party, held just seventeen days before the poll (due on 27th July), and with the campaign already under way, a frail George Edwards was persuaded to stand: "the motion carried with the greatest enthusiasm, with everyone standing and cheering to the echo". Edwin Gooch was his "faithful agent" again and immediately set up a Fighting Fund.

Edwards had a radical programme for agriculture: national ownership of land, a standard living wage, statutory working week, abolition of the tied cottage, and land for smallholdings to be easily and cheaply obtained. A great gathering was held in Wymondham. He was met at the station by the band of the Discharged Soldiers and Sailors Federation who "played me up to the Fairland, the place of meeting, where there were upwards of 1,500 people waiting to receive me, and I was given a wonderful reception".

On polling day things did not go so swimmingly. The candidate's tour of the constituency with Mr Gooch and Mr Taylor got as far as Shotesham Common, where the Labour Party car broke down. After a three hour wait for a replacement their progress resumed.

However, the rural electorate, perhaps sensing their power for the first time, swept "Our George" to Westminster with a majority of 2,118 over the Coalition candidate Mr Batty. The Union's new monthly journal the Land Worker was jubilant: "A Great Victory in South Norfolk. The Union's Man Romps Home".

Mr and Mrs Gooch—Edwin was "the organiser of the victory"; Ethel was Vice-President of the South Norfolk Party from May 1920—were in the group that accompanied a triumphant George Edwards to London by the 9am train. In the Land Worker Taylor exulted: "We had a time! Conscious that nobody less than a full-blown MP was in our midst, we were as large as any of the swell Cockneys... 'the goods'

George Edwards and his agent Edwin Gooch outside the Labour Institute in Wymondham after his by-election victory in South Norfolk, 1920.

delivered from South Norfolk, all 'spic and span' in a brand new suit..." (In *Sharpen the Sickle*, the first history of the NUAW, Reg Groves claims it was "a suit that had been passed on to a union man by a charitable peer of the district", presumably Kimberley.)

They cheered from the Strangers' Gallery as "our Ploughman" took the oath in the House (treading on Lloyd George's toe in the process), as one of his fellow-Labour MPs called out "Good old farmer's boy!" Edwards was the first farmworker to go to the Commons as a Labour member—Joseph Arch, also originally a farmworker, had been Liberal MP for North-West Norfolk. Arch had died in 1919 so did not witness this repeat of his success. George was welcomed home to Fakenham by the town band playing *See The Conquering Hero Comes*.

Back in Wymondham, Edwin Gooch stepped down as Honorary Agent, perhaps to the relief of his editor at the *Mercury*, but nevertheless his political work expanded. He was nominated as a magistrate but was refused "owing to political intervention from the other side". In December 1920 Edwin was selected to represent the division at a special Labour Party national conference on Ireland (where civil war was raging) and Ethel was a delegate to a Commonwealth League Conference in Norwich in May 1921, intending to vote for the nationalisation of land when the Labour Party came to power.

In January 1922 Edwin moved that George Edwards, the sitting MP, be nominated again as the candidate for South Norfolk; Tom Higdon of Burston seconded: "Resolution carried with much enthusiasm and musical honours were accorded". George addressed the crowd at Wymondham's Labour Day, as reported in the local press: "He denounced the arch-deceiver Lloyd George and was in fine political tub-thumping form, and

Edwin Gooch, journalist, entering the political fray, 1920s.

worked in all his 'old chestnuts' to such an extent that he had to use them with apologies for their antiquity".

There was a brief fuss in the correspondence columns of the *Eastern Daily Press* during the 1922 General Election campaign. One unsigned letter (but its style possibly showing the hand of Edwin Gooch) responded to another reader's complaint about Labour supporters disrupting Sunday services in Wymondham: "'Sunday School Teacher' raves about the brass bands and noisy processions. Why? Labour demonstration! Had it been a friendly society on church parade, a regiment of soldiers with all the accursed trappings of militarism, Boy Scouts or Church Lads' Brigade with their intolerable drums and bugles it would have been 'all right'".

The November 1922 cover of the *Land Worker* emphasised to apprehensive rural supporters of Labour that "THE BALLOT ☞ IS SECRET", but despite the help of a new full-time agent, and increasing his share, Edwards lost this time by 861 votes to a Unionist candidate.

The Land Worker

with which is incorporated "The Labourer"

OFFICIAL ORGAN OF THE NATIONAL UNION OF AGRICULTURAL WORKERS.

| VOL. 3 No. 42. | [Subscription for 12 months including postage. 3s.] | NOVEMBER, 1922. | [Postage: United Kingdom, 1d. Foreign and Colonial, 1d.] | PRICE 2d. |

NOVEMBER 15th, 1922

Labour Candidate | X

THE BALLOT
☞ IS SECRET

Front cover of the Land Worker, for the November 1922 Election when George Edwards lost his South Norfolk seat.

Tom Higdon of the Burston Strike School was a major figure in the NUAW and the South Norfolk Labour Party in the 1920s and 1930s.

Stand by the Old Union Ship

IN 1922, after "years devoted to spade work for the Party", Edwin Gooch was elected to a multiplicity of offices—a local breakthrough for Labour described as "phenomenal" by the press: County Councillor (for the Hingham Division), Rural District Councillor (for Forehoe District), Poor Law Guardian and Parish Councillor (for Wymondham). He was appointed a Justice of the Peace in October 1922 after being blocked since 1920 by his political opponents.

The local prominence these roles gave Edwin was, nevertheless, no preparation for a dramatic turn of events in Norfolk.

Farming had been plunged into depression after the Conservative/Liberal Coalition ended the wartime financial guarantees in June 1921, panicked by a big drop in world prices and the prospect that they would have to subsidise agriculture on an uncontrollably vast scale. The free market did indeed have a catastrophic effect, but on farmers and farmworkers rather than the Exchequer: wheat prices halved in six months, beef by forty per cent, and land was everywhere taken out of production.

In a "Great Betrayal"—despite earlier confirmation by Lloyd George of the existing arrangements in the 1920 Agriculture Act—the wartime Central Wages Board went, too, at the end of September 1921, in the wake of the harvest. It was replaced by local Conciliation Committees. These comprised equal numbers of farmers and workers, with an independent chairman, but being entirely voluntary were therefore without authority. So farming became a brutal free-for-all as farmers struggled to survive: a return to seasonal lay-offs and arbitrary 'master and man' relations. Wages were cut savagely, from a high point of 46/- a week in 1920 to 25/- in 1923. The unions, seemingly impotent, suffered a rapid fall in membership: the National Union of Agricultural Workers was about a fifth of its immediate post-war size, and in effect retreated to its Norfolk heartland, "the test county for the whole country".

In January 1922 in the so-called 'Sack of Wheat' dispute, two hundred or so farmworkers went on strike in West Norfolk on a huge 7,000 acre estate whose owner had wanted to peg wages to the price of wheat. The issue was resolved in April that year when the farmer agreed to abide by Conciliation Committee decisions in future. Though this might have seemed like a Union victory, it was only a brief respite, as wages were still falling across the county. In

33

this time of ever-increasing tension the Norfolk NUAW Secretary, Sam Peel, incurred the wrath of General Secretary Robert Walker— somewhat isolated from events—for unilaterally accepting a 30/- wage at a Conciliation Committee meeting, despite its 7 to 1 rejection by the Norfolk County Committee.

The NUAW's Biennial Conference, held in London in June 1922, resolved to re-establish the Agricultural Wages Board, to fix a minimum wage and a 48-hour week. Edwin Gooch, like a majority of his Norfolk colleagues, had been for conciliation in order to achieve these aims, giving his opinion that "they would get better terms than by uttering threats against the farmers". Tom Higdon urged that they should

Sam Peel, a dedicated public servant in Norfolk all his life, took an independent line in wage negotiations for the NUAW in 1923.

decide clearly on conciliation or fighting. Walter Smith, the NUAW President, was concerned that "so many members were threatening they would not pay any more money into the Union because they had been sold".

Edwin—despite objecting to Sam Peel's lack of consultation—had been his ally, as well as a friend. But Peel, a Quaker and undoubtedly a man of true public-spiritedness, made the decision to resign from the NUAW. He formed a breakaway National Union of Land Workers soon after, backed by the farmers.

This was too much for Edwin Gooch and most others in Norfolk. It threatened the very existence of the National Union of Agricultural Workers and forced members to take sides. George Edwards appealed to the wavering County Committee and the Norfolk membership to "Stick to the Union that has stood by you". In the *Land Worker* W.B.Taylor urged members to "stand by the old Union ship".

At a meeting in July 1922 Bro.Gooch moved a resolution designed to clear up any doubts, and thus nailed his colours to the mast: "That we desire to place on record our appreciation of the work of the NUAW in its attempts to raise the status of the agricultural labourer and to secure for him a greater share of the fruits of his labour. We endorse the general conciliatory policy of the Union

Executive, and call upon the agricultural labourers of the county to remain loyal to the Union". It was carried unanimously.

Edwin Gooch's closeness to Edwards (as a skilled sub-editor he'd been asked by George to put his autobiography *From Crow-Scaring to Westminster* "into shape") would have outweighed any residual sympathy for Peel, who became a hate figure at the time for the Union rank and file. An exchange of letters between Peel and Gooch in the *Eastern Daily Press* in March 1923 concerned Peel's stance in taking a personal initiative on the wage negotiation and setting up his "dummy" union, dismissed by Edwin as wishful thinking.

Despite this public falling out, the two former colleagues—both Wymondham men—continued to cooperate on Norfolk County Council in the realms of Health and Education, and with time their friendship resumed. A photo in the *Land Worker* for June 1948 showed Edwin Gooch and "Mr Sam Peel of the Society of Friends" at the grave of their mutual friend Sir George Edwards, who had also been reconciled to Peel. Susan Wild, in her biography of her grandfather—*Sam Peel, A Man Who Did Different*—makes clear what a great force for public good he was in North Norfolk. She concludes that Peel had made a serious error of judgment in 1922; in his attempt to put pressure on the Government by bringing farmers and farmworkers together he had underestimated the desperate condition of the men. It could be argued that it was Edwin Gooch who shared Sam Peel's philosophy but learned from his tactical mistake.

In this entrenched situation in the dispute, conciliation seemed to be a thing of the past. The Norfolk farmers pushed for a further cut of, in effect, 2/6d a week, plus an extra four hours' work. Edwards, who in his autobiography had claimed he always had "the greatest horror of a strike, and would go to almost any length to prevent it", now wrote *A Call to My Comrades* in the *Land Worker* of February 1923: "The moment has arrived..."

There was one last attempt to bring the Government in to restore reasonable standards. National Union of Agricultural Workers, Workers Union and National Farmers Union delegations visited the Prime Minister Bonar Law together at 10 Downing Street, on 16th March, but came away empty-handed. The Prime Minister, repeatedly challenged by Walker, simply stated that nothing could be done. George Edwards declared "It was like giving us mustard without any beef".

In the Spring of 1923, with the sowing of that year's crops an urgent priority, the crunch came. The NUAW, though the fall in membership had virtually reduced it to a rump, decided to strike in Norfolk (thereby risking bankruptcy) to halt the run of cruel wage cuts. The national Executive Committee resolved on 5th March that "no settlement should be made lower than the standard prevailing when the men came out"; and on the 29th March: "This Executive of the NUAW after fully considering the terrible plight of the agricultural worker and his family since the destruction of the Wages Board calls upon the Government to declare the industry a sweated trade and immediately bring the workers engaged therein within the scope of the Trade Boards Act".

Even at the time it was thought that the National Farmers' Union may have engineered the confrontation to force the Government to reinstate support for agriculture, or at least saw potential leverage in the situation as deadlock ensued around 'seedtime', in mid-April. According to the writer H. Rider Haggard, farming his estate at Ditchingham, it was "'put up' or planned". The National Union of Agricultural Workers seems to have seen this as the only way, too, but had to fight for its place at the table.

The Great Strike

THE 'Great Strike' began sporadically, with a few hundred men locked out while both sides waited on developments elsewhere. The Ministry of Agriculture brought the two sides together in a conference at the Shire Hall in Norwich, when the farmers' best offer was 25/- for 53 hours. This was rejected and the lock-outs spread. A week later, on the 24th March, a second session, under the auspices of the Bishop of Norwich, got nowhere, despite farmers' and workers' representatives lunching together in the Bishop's Palace. The National Union of Agricultural Workers' declared lowest position was 26/- for 50 hours. All these wage offers, in contrast to the wartime premium, were at subsistence level.

That night, 24th March, the strike was officially on. All Norfolk members were called out, though this was modified later to all farms where the pay was less than 30/- for 50 hours, and later 26/- for 50 hours. In the event only a quarter of the county membership joined—mainly from the big farms of the west, south-west and the north—and numbers varied from 6,000 to 10,000.

As a member of the NUAW's Emergency Committee, Edwin Gooch (who had the newborn Michael at home) was elected Treasurer of the Distress Fund, in charge of the hundreds of pounds contributed daily from all over Britain. Strike headquarters was Keir Hardie Hall, Norwich, where James Lunnon, National Organizing Secretary, having come up from London on his motorcycle

Edwin and Ethel Gooch with baby Michael, born just a couple of months before the Great Strike in 1923.

to take charge, spoke under a large engraving of John Wesley preaching. A printed memo was sent out to all branches: "Get collecting boxes made... the proceeds, after paying expenses, sent to Mr Gooch, the treasurer".

Another leaflet, probably the work of the journalist Edwin Gooch, urged: "Don't let the burden on the labourers' homes be heavier than the wives can bear. The men are in great spirit and can look after themselves. Help us to look after the wives and the little ones... We appeal for support to every lover of justice in the County. Make this the Treasurer's best week-end. Remember that every penny so collected goes EXCLUSIVELY to the Distress Fund. Help Now. It's NOW we want it! All contributions to E.G.GOOCH, Treasurer, 'Rydal Mount', Wymondham, or Hardie Hall, St Gregory's Alley, Norwich."

Strike pay was 12/- a week for a married man, and 6d for each child, or 6/- for a single man, disbursed via branch officials, but no one could survive on this subsistence rate for long. The Labour movement gave financial support, in particular the NUR, whose members in an era of branch lines (and in Norfolk the rambling Midland & Great Northern Railway) often had direct links to rural communities. George Lansbury MP, writing in his paper the *Daily Herald*, urged "Give everything you can and give it quickly".

A mass-meeting was held in Norwich Market Place on April 9th, after talks held that day at the Shire Hall were adjourned. Two processions, marching behind the Buckenham Brass Band and the St Faith's Band, converged. James Lunnon spoke, as did E.G.Gooch. A press photo shows a great crowd of men in flat caps. Walker wrote that "the whole action of the farmers could only be explained as an attempt to force the government to give more concessions to the farm employers". In fact the Government fell that very day, and a General Election loomed.

Out in the countryside the strike was a confused affair of "cycle scouts"—the original flying pickets—and skirmishes between columns of strikers (many of them ex-servicemen wearing their medal ribbons) on "route marches" and young blackleg middle-class volunteers recruited by the maverick Farmers' Federation. Horses were unyoked in the fields and blows were exchanged between strikers and blacklegs. The press overstated these incidents in the Norfolk countryside, though the Union was doing its best to keep the roving pickets under control. George Edwards was doubtful: "these men have the war spirit, and however much I regret this spirit, I am sure it is going to show itself if this dispute continues for another ten days".

Such tensions across the class divide were, in some ways, a rural dress rehearsal for the 1926 General Strike, but often the atmosphere was more farcical than confrontational. Edwin later reported to Conference that: "Those who were strangers to Norfolk, seeing there were 600 summonses issued, thought that the Norfolk labourers on strike were the biggest scoundrels on earth. But summonses were applied for and issued on very paltry grounds... There were imported into the County of Norfolk some hundreds of policemen from outside, who spent most of their time joy-riding about the country in char-a-bancs".

In one incident, twenty-five strikers charged with intimidation were to be brought before the Bench at Walsingham. On the appointed day ten Labour-

Walsingham, during the Great Strike, where the Labour-supporting JPs (including Edwin Gooch) "crammed the bench". This postcard records George Edwards's cry of "Be good lads!" when the crowd threatened Sam Peel.

supporting JPs, including Edwin Gooch, drove up to the Old Courthouse, joining and outnumbering the local magistrates and thus ensuring leniency. After this coup there was a "riot" in the square as strikers tried to set upon Sam Peel JP and pelted him with rotten fruit and vegetables; police and the Labour magistrates intervened to protect him and a postcard of the scuffle was circulated with George Edwards's cry of concern, "Be good lads!", inscribed.

The front cover of the *Land Worker* for April 1923 had an uncompromising headline: "The Farm War". Below it was a photograph of the Norfolk Dispute Committee formed up outside Keir Hardie Hall in Norwich, including James Lunnon, George Edwards, George Hewitt, Edwin Gooch and Tom Higdon. (Beneath the photo is a soothing advert for Bourneville Cocoa.) Inside a reporter asks a striker "How long are you ready to stay out?"; he replies "Until I starve".

That issue's stirring leader, under the title *Norfolk's Brilliant Lead—A Fight for Hearth and Home*, was written by E.G.Gooch: "I had begun to despair of the Norfolk labourers. The men had grown indifferent as to their present and future welfare... The wages had dropped from 46s to 25s a week. A year since they were committed to a 30s wage despite a 7 to 1 vote against acceptance of the same. The full story of how the men were sold on that occasion still remains to be told. Suffice to say the Union is now clear of such influence... 'We might as well starve for a time without work as to starve for all time at work'... The Norfolk labourer

OFFICIAL ORGAN OF THE NATIONAL UNION OF AGRICULTURAL WORKERS.

VOL. 4. No. 47. [Subscription for 12 months including postage, 3s.]   APRIL, 1923.   [Postage: United Kingdom, 1d. Foreign and Colonial, ½d.]   PRICE 2d.

THE FARM WAR.

Photo by courtesy of the *Norwich Mercury*.

Members of the Norfolk Dispute Committee of the National Union of Agricultural Workers and other County leaders concerned in the conduct of the men's case, photographed outside their headquarters at Norwich. Reading from left to right they are (sitting) Messrs. J. A. Arnett, J. Lunnon, George Edwards, G. E. Hewitt, and E. G. Gooch. (Standing) Messrs. H. E. Durham, R. A. Watson, H. Harvey, A. Holness, P. Rounce, J. Weatherbed, J. Etheridge, J. Coe, J. Pightling, and T. G. Higdon. (Councillor W. R. Taylor, a member of the Committee, is not in the above group.)

Front cover of the Land Worker, April 1923: 'The Farm War', showing the Norfolk Strike Committee outside Keir Hardie Hall, Norwich. George Edwards sits at centre, with Edwin Gooch sitting far right, and Tom Higdon standing far right.

is a born fighter... On 25s the labourer is down and out, and the public knows it and wants him to win and lift himself above the poverty line. Will the labourer win? He must and he will. The mantle of Kett and Arch has descended upon him. His sun is rising and best of all, God is on his side".

Another published photograph from April 1923 shows striking farmworkers marching from Wicklewood Workhouse, near Wymondham, where they had demanded relief and food from the Parish Guardians, to a rally in the grounds of Kimberley Hall; they are carrying the banner of the old NUALRW and Edwin Gooch and other Union men stand at the head of the procession. The Guardians agreed to grant relief "in goods" to needy cases, causing the *Land Worker* to declare: "The men's action 'put the wind up' the employers. They were afraid it would be imitated all over the county and the whole Poor Law disorganised. Probably this helped substantially towards the settlement".

Strikers march on Wicklewood Workhouse, near Wymondham, requesting outdoor relief, 1923. Edwin Gooch stands to the right, in front of the old Mulbarton NUALRW banner.

The resolution of an increasingly bitter dispute came, in effect, when Labour's leader Ramsay MacDonald—himself the son of a farm labourer—brought the two sides together in the House of Commons on April 18th. Harry Gosling, President of the all-powerful Transport & General Workers Union, lent his influential support. The Union deputation hurried back to Norfolk and the members of the County Emergency Committee were summoned to Keir Hardie Hall by telegram. Strongly influenced by MacDonald's and Gosling's recommendation, they agreed to accept the NFU's terms. There was no generosity at all from the farmers, but in settling for a subsistence level wage of 25/- and a 50-hour week the NUAW claimed to have at least "stopped the rot". In a "Hallelujah Wind-up" to the strike *The Red Flag* was sung with pride in Keir Hardie Hall.

The harsh fact remained that this was five shillings less than the sum that had been on offer through Sam Peel's one-man initiative (which might not, of course, have been honoured). This was not lost on the Union's Executive Committee, nor on Edwin. It was clear that there were limits to what could be achieved by industrial action in the countryside.

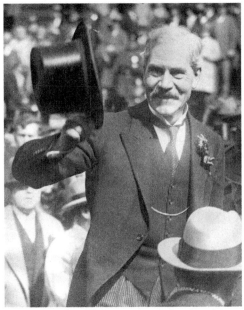

Ramsay Macdonald visiting New York as Britain's first Labour Prime Minister — a photo from Edwin Gooch's scrapbook.

Treasurer Edwin Gooch had paid out £35,000 to the men in about four weeks, and the NUAW was virtually bankrupt.

Edwin Gooch's conciliatory role in the period after the Great Strike has been criticised by some later writers as being too close to the discredited policy of Peel, though Edwin had been at his most pugnacious during the strike. His comments in the sometimes ugly aftermath in response to threats by the farmers (who had signed up to "no victimisation") show that he was far from passive, and make clear his passionate Methodism-derived Socialist ethos: "...that a country which calls itself Christian should tolerate such a state of affairs passes my comprehension..."

He continued the theme at a Labour Rally at Hingham on April 30th 1923, as reported in the *Eastern Daily Press*: "Despite the present ugly feature [*victimisation of strikers by farmers*], they must regard the settlement as a victory for the workers. The labourers had now established a position for themselves and had stopped the rot. Those still off the farms must not get themselves in a panic. The union was behind them and would see them through. He warned the farmers that serious consequences would follow their present unsportsmanlike attitude".

Despite this continuing evidence of bad faith, Edwin Gooch took the long view when speaking at the Pelican Inn, Tacolnestone: "He could assure the other side that if they were building their hopes of smashing the men's union by such a method they were doomed to disappointment (Hear, hear)... The labourers were going forward to greater things for their class. With the backing of the entire Labour movement of the country they were going to secure themselves a measure of security and justice which had long been denied them". Perhaps inevitably, NUAW branch secretaries seem to have suffered most prejudice from their employers; Edwin described them as "marked men".

Edwin Gooch's vision of a better future, sustained by his instinct for consensus and "sweet reasonableness" in the George Edwards mould, was shared in some measure by almost all parties to these events—in particular Ramsay MacDonald, now head of the second largest party in Parliament. His intervention, apparently prompted by a pragmatic desire to move away from "class war" and be seen as the peacemaker in an industrial dispute, with an election coming and the imminent prospect of national power for Labour, had led to the settlement that ended the Norfolk Great Strike. MacDonald himself visited Wymondham in July 1923, a few months after the strike ended, perhaps as a nod towards his old comrade George Edwards and the coming man in the Union, Edwin Gooch.

In the December 1923 General Election, George Edwards, his support perhaps buoyed by the spirit of solidarity of the Great Strike, reversed the South Norfolk result of November 1922 with a majority of 861. The septuagenarian "farmer's boy" was back at Westminster.

In the South Norfolk Minutes "gratification was expressed on the accession to power of the Labour Party"; the national result, however, had been close, and Ramsay MacDonald could govern only as minority, supported by the Liberals.

In its nine months of existence, the first Labour Government's main achievement was a Housing Act that increased the subsidy to local authorities for building homes, and an Agricultural Wages (Regulation) Act (established county by county) to restore the minimum wage for farmworkers that had been lost in 1921—the very issue that had lead to the Great Strike.

Edwin Gooch, becoming a prominent figure in the NUAW in the wake of the Great Strike, as well as on Norfolk County Council.

Our County Work

EDWIN Gooch was a Norfolk delegate to the 1924 National Union of Agricultural Workers' Biennial Conference in London where, brimming with battle-hardened confidence, he made a flurry of speeches, in one of which he boasted that Norfolk was "the strongest link in the chain... We keep the organisation going". Perhaps feeling somewhat overenthusiastic, he proposed a string of resolutions, all of which were lost. The most eye-catching in the light of the future of the NUAW was his surprisingly pessimistic proposal to amalgamate with the Workers' Union (affiliated to the Transport & General Workers Union), to prevent the Union continuing on "a downward road... in a very short space of time there would be no union at all".

He spoke against a resolution to limit Executive Committee membership to "no-one but bona-fide agricultural workers". The minutes record: "He [Bro. Gooch] said it would deprive him of one of the pleasures of his life, of going every Monday to assist the agricultural workers of his county. He was not one of those individuals who had sought office; he had simply offered his services. He was not an agricultural worker, although in his early days he used to nail the shoes on the horses... [the resolution] would deprive not only him but hundreds of other people of the opportunity... to keep the Union going". This was an effective intervention: the resolution was lost, thereby allowing him to continue his increasingly prominent role in the Union. Edwin's professional distance from agriculture protected him from victimisation; as Professor Alun Howkins noted, this was "a real strength".

George Edwards was again proposed by Edwin Gooch as South Norfolk candidate for the October 1924 General Election, but Edwards lost his seat to the Unionist James Christie. The 'Red Letter' Election was to some extent fixed by the forged 'Zinoviev letter' published in the *Daily Mail* that seemed to implicate Labour in pro-Soviet initiatives and even preparations for Bolshevik revolution in Britain. The first Labour Government's brief term in office was over after they lost forty of their 191 seats.

The following February Edwards, by then in his mid-seventies, announced that he would be bowing out of parliamentary politics. His speech to the South Norfolk EC was reported in the press: "...his heart beat as true as ever for the cause. He had not sheathed the sword nor soiled the flag in the mud, but he wanted to say that the arm that bore the sword was beginning to be weary, and the head that carried the helmet wanted rest". Clearly there was a need for a younger man to take up the fight.

In June 1925 George Edwards formally resigned as the prospective parliamentary candidate. A newspaper clipping preserved in the South Norfolk Labour Party Minutes marked "GEORGE'S FAREWELL: May the declining years of the fine old toiler be many and happy, and the evening of his days be peace..."

Edwin and Ethel Gooch, George Edwards and fellow-delegates—including the tall Hugh Dalton MP. Labour Party Conference, Brighton, late 1920s.

A year later Edwin Gooch, in presenting an Illuminated Address (and the sum of £45) to his mentor, described how George Edwards "joined the little band of timid souls who in 1918 ventured upon the extremely unpopular step of forming a new party in South Norfolk"; a press photo of the time shows Edwards and a jovial group of supporters, including Edwin, outside Beckett's Chapel in Wymondham, with the framed Address.

NUAW delegates at the same Labour Party Conference, Brighton, late 1920s. Seated to Edwin's right is Bill Holmes, General Secretary. Behind George Edwards is his niece Elizabeth.

It seems that Edwards had been grooming Edwin Gooch as a successor in the Union and the Party for some time. They shared a strong Primitive Methodist faith and Socialist principles, though without rigid ideology. Alun Howkins, in his entry for Edwin Gooch in the *Dictionary of National Biography* considered that Edwards' two electoral victories: "...clearly owed a very great deal to

The Norfolk County Banner at a Union demonstration, with Edwin Gooch, George Edwards and Tom Higdon.

Gooch who was able to marshal the farmworkers' vote, a potentially large but politically disorganised majority of the electorate". It was only six years since Edwin and Ethel Gooch and others had set up the South Norfolk Labour Party, but that time had been packed with drama and incident. Gooch and Edwards had become close through the parliamentary and Union battles, and early on in their relationship George Edwards seems to have recognised in Edwin, with his sound and steady character and clear way with words, a future leader.

After the strike: unwinding but not undressing on the beach at Cromer. Edwin is holding his nephew Peter; Pat Banham is holding Michael Gooch.

Edwin was certainly very active locally in the wake of the Great Strike, as the Union tried to improve the terms agreed, but relations between farmer and farmworker were still troubled. On 10th February 1926 the Executive Committee of the NUAW in London received a telegram from Norfolk: "Our resolution for increase defeated. Present rates continue. Gooch". It was decided to call a delegate conference in Norwich on the 27th to protest against "inhuman starvation wages". This resulted in a plan for a ballot of Norfolk members whether to cease work, but no strike action ensued. Was this simply exhaustion after the struggles of 1923?

The General Strike in May 1926 did not directly involve the farmworkers, who were not called upon by the Trades Union Congress, but the NUAW made a grant of £2000 to striking miners. The strike's failure after eight days led to a broad shift in trade union policy away from confrontation. Restrictive measures enacted by Baldwin's Tory Government in its aftermath, via the Trade Disputes and Trade Unions Act of 1927, made large-scale sympathetic strikes illegal and heavily penalised picketing.

Edwin Gooch—County Councillor for the Hingham division since 1922—was proposed as the Westminster candidate for South Norfolk in June 1926, but demurred: "...the position of an MP did not appeal to him in the very least. He would rather continue to be useful in Norfolk than to be buried alive in London, and it gave him more pleasure to administer relief to the poor in the Forehoe Union than it would do to become a mere cog in the Parliamentary machine".

When the salary of the constituency agent was no longer paid by Lord Kimberley, George Young, who offered to pay half the agent's salary himself, became the prospective candidate. (South Norfolk had plenty of other expenses to cover in these busy years, including £17/5/9 for repairs to a Citroen and a Humber, £3 to the Buckenham Band, but only a "thanks for their services" to the Gem Orchestra.)

In 1926 Edwin Gooch was profiled in a local newspaper series "Men and Women in the Public Eye, Sketches of Norfolk and Suffolk Notabilities". His rapid rise to public prominence and elected office in the county was considered phenomenal for a man "still on the sunny side of forty". He was already involved in a long list of committees and sub-committees on the County Council —where "ability is soon recognised": Education, County Finance, Public Health, Eastern Highways, Selection, Office Accommodation, Tuberculosis, Blind Persons, County Library, Printing, Old Age Pensions, County Rates etc. He was also a visitor to H.M. Prison, Norwich; a Governor of King Edward VI School, Norwich; and was on the Council of the Norfolk County Playing Fields Association. All this as well as continuing to hold down his job as sub-editor on the *Mercury*.

In a Norfolk County Council electoral address quoted in the article, Alderman Waters, Father of the Council, was warm in his non-partisan praise for Edwin: "For the past three years you have been my colleague, and I should much regret your absence from the new council. Many practical proposals have been made by you. More often than not the position you took I could cordially approve. Whenever our views were not the same yours were certain to be such as to command my respect. There is a growing future for you in our County work... and I trust the voters to give you a sound majority. If I were an elector in your division you would have my vote, not on political grounds, but because of your independence, ability, and fairness to those from whom you may differ".

Edwin Gooch had worked at his father's forge in earlier days, then "laying down the smith's hammer he picked up the compositor's stick, and after a period as a printer he passed into journalism". In a paragraph sub-headed *Home Influences* Edwin was modest: "...much of the success that has come to him in the directions indicated is attributable to his mother (long since passed away), who guided his footsteps aright in early life, the religious and moral training he received as a youth in the ranks of

Ethel Gooch was also becoming a public figure, sitting on Norfolk County Council from the 1920s.

Ethel Gooch attends a women's meeting in Wymondham, General Election 1929?

Primitive Methodism and Rechabitism, and the sympathetic and practical interest taken in all that he undertakes by his wife".

Ethel had left off teaching after their son Michael was born in 1923, but this was just the beginning of a life of public service and local political activism to rival her husband's. Like Edwin she took on a multiplicity of honorary roles in the 1920s and 1930s, as a councillor for Forehoe District, a Norfolk County Councillor and Chair of the Maternity and Welfare Committee, later an Alderman and JP. To help sustain this busy political and administrative life the Goochs employed a servant girl while Michael was small, and a part-time gardener. Michael would also be routinely looked after by Ethel's sister Mabel, married to Walter Lane, and living above his gentleman's outfitters shop opposite the Wymondham Methodist Church. Ethel was celebrated for being so distracted by political and public affairs that she could neglect immediate practical concerns. On one famous occasion she was so busy talking business while pouring tea into a cups at a Women's Institute meeting that she filled three imaginary ones beyond the end of the row!

South Norfolk Parliamentary Election, 1931

GIVE LABOUR POWER

**National Re-construction
without Food Taxes.**

TARIFFS mean a **BREAD TAX**
and **LESS WAGES** for all.

VOTE

FOR

GOOCH

The 1931 Election was one of Labour's worst defeats, back to their 1910 position, after Ramsay MacDonald formed a National Government with the Conservatives.

Lift Up the Great Banner of Labour

FROM June 1926 Edwin Gooch sat on the National Union of Agricultural Workers' Executive Committee, having come top of the ballot at that year's Biennial, thus marking a significant shift from a local to a national role.

In August 1928 there was suddenly a vacuum to fill in the NUAW leadership. General Secretary Bob Walker emigrated to Australia, perhaps disillusioned by the state of Labour politics, and Bill Holmes moved across from the Presidency. Edwin was proposed for President by George Edwards, who declined to stand himself. Tom Higdon, George Hewitt and other stalwarts also stood, but it was the relative newcomer Edwin Gooch who was voted in as temporary Chairman, though he accepted with the caveat that he "would not automatically be willing to stand for President".

Edwin Gooch, temporary Chairman from 1928, then President of the NUAW from 1930.

In March 1929 Edwin Gooch gave up his position as Secretary to the South Norfolk party, after ten years of keeping the Minutes. The General Election in May that year (following the extension of the franchise to all women over the age of twenty-one) brought in another precarious Labour government. They were the largest party now, but without an overall majority and thus dependent again on Lloyd George's Liberals. Noel Buxton, Labour MP for North Norfolk, was made Minister of Agriculture.

After the Unionist James Christie's defeat of Labour's George Young in South Norfolk (though by a smaller margin than George Edwards' five years earlier), Edwin Gooch criticised the loser at a local Executive Committee meeting:

51

South Norfolk election meeting at Diss, 1931. Tom Higdon in the chair, with the candidate Edwin Gooch.

"Neither the candidate nor the agent were in the confidence of the Party, Mr Young did not make friends with the people, nor could he, what the Party needed was a man who could lead".

That man was in fact Edwin Gooch, who finally accepted the nomination in October 1929. According to the Minutes: "George Edwards took Edwin Gooch by the hand and bade him lift up the great banner of Labour that South Norfolk might return to the old faith (Applause)".

The *Norfolk Chronicle* reported the adoption meeting in January 1930 and profiled the candidate: "Although only forty years of age Mr Gooch's rise in public life in the county has been almost meteoric, and today he is one of the best-known men in public affairs in Norfolk." It went on to list his numerous local roles in Wymondham, Forehoe District and Norfolk County, and for the Labour Party and National Union of Agricultural Workers: "He is a member of the Labour Party's Agricultural Advisory Committee, and is now serving as a workers' representative to the Agricultural Conference convened by the Government. Since the re-establishment of the Agricultural Wages Board, Mr Gooch has been the men's leader on the Norfolk Wages Committee". As well as these representative positions he was also the ex-President of Wymondham Co-operative Society, a member of the Justices' Visiting Committee to Norwich Prison, a governor of King Edward VI School, Norwich, and of Hingham

Grammar School. Mrs Gooch likewise played a prominent role in the district, including as a governor of her old school, East Dereham High.

"Mr Gooch, in reply, said he was deeply conscious of the honour the party had done him in asking him to become their candidate. It was a job entirely unsought for on his part, and one that he took on with considerable reluctance. That was the second time of asking. On a former occasion he declined the honour mainly on the ground that he desired to continue uninterrupted his public work locally."

He ended on an optimistic note: "Do I need to tell you that I am a thorough-going Labour man? I have never hidden my light under a bushel. I am devoted to my party and its leaders. The party is sound and honest and is the one medium through which abundant prosperity will return to this country, and the workers enjoy the full fruits of their labour. Our leaders are men of integrity and honour who excel in the art of government... Five years of Tory muddle and mismanagement have left their mark, but the Augean stable is being cleaned out, and a period of Labour government without full power will be followed by a more fruitful period with complete power."

Edwin Gooch was by now unequivocally a man of the political middle ground, the Centre-Left in current terms. In 1929 he spoke to the Dorchester branch of the NUAW, insisting that the farmworker was not the farmer's natural enemy; he would be his ally if given the opportunity: "We are not against conference with the employer on a broad national basis". But his speech to the 1930 NUAW Biennial also highlighted the continuing scandal of rural housing: "In many an old-world cottage with its pretty thatched roof and roses round the door lurk often such enemies as rheumatism and consumption"; the union would not cease its agitation until the last tied cottage tenant was freed.

Despite his expressed reservations, Edwin was voted NUAW President at the 1930 Conference, an honorary but highly influential position that he was to hold until his death.

Alun Howkins wrote of this key moment in the Union's history in his *DNB* profile:

"Gooch's election marked an important change in the direction of the Union and its policy, which was aided by the resignation in 1928 of Robert Walker as Secretary. Walker represented an older, more radical and avowedly socialist position, which was increasingly undermined by declining union membership, widespread and growing unemployment and what was seen by many on the Executive as the failure of the 'militant' policy of 1923 and afterwards. Against this Gooch proposed a policy of moderation which was essentially based on a belief that agriculture as a sector of the economy should be united, with farmworkers, farmers and landowners working together. In Gooch's view a successful and prosperous agriculture would automatically lead to prosperity for the farm worker. This meant an end to the 'class war in the countryside' which many wrote about in the 1920s and its replacement with a policy of cooperation within the industry with wages and conditions mediated through the peaceful means of the government run wages boards."

Edwin Gooch, as NUAW President, was non-confrontational by conviction (Christian "brotherly love" was fundamental and impartial), with a belief that legislation and industrial co-operation were most likely to provide real protection for a vulnerable workforce, as they had during the 1914-18 war. The Labour Government of 1924 had reinstated the Central Wages Board, but this did not as yet have "teeth". Edwin's consensual politics slowly proved effective, leading to higher wages, paid holidays and unemployment insurance for farm workers; Alun Howkins concluded that he "guided the NUAW through the difficult years of the 1930s with studied moderation".

The tone for his long period of tenure seems to have been set by a Government-convened Agricultural Conference in 1931, where delegates from the National Union of Agricultural Workers and the National Farmers Union met. Edwin Gooch, still a professional journalist, was in attendance as President, photographed in a bowler hat and spats. The discussions were confidential, but would become public two years later amid allegations of the farmers' bad faith, showing the limitations of a collegiate approach in that era.

Edwin's mood at the time, as expressed in a *Land Worker* article, was pessimistic: "All parties met in a spirit of goodwill but the conference demonstrated that it was well nigh impossible to reconcile the interests in agriculture". But he persevered. An editorial, "A Common Meeting Ground", announced the new President's policy shift to the centre in 1931. In the teeth of the Depression, any more confrontational line would have been highly impractical. Not only that, but mechanisation of agriculture was already undermining the Union's strength.

Perhaps only the very unlikely prospect of Soviet-style collectivisation (much discussed in the *Land Worker* in those years) or a government-financed version of the New Deal, could have prevented or postponed the decline of trade union power in the countryside in the long run—though in fact NUAW numbers would reach their peak in the post-Second World War decade.

The economic crisis in the wake of the 1929 Wall Street Crash meant that the farmworkers were suddenly very vulnerable again. Ramsay MacDonald and his Chancellor Philip Snowden opted for wage and benefit cuts, supported by the Conservatives, and ten Labour ministers resigned on the issue after an ultimatum from the Bank of England. On August 31st 1931 a National Government was formed, chiefly of Conservatives and Liberals, with MacDonald staying on as Prime Minister. Labour's 261 MPs became the official Opposition, under George Lansbury. It was a bitter split, and MacDonald has not been forgiven to this day.

The Depression deepened, the United Kingdom left the Gold Standard and Sterling lost 20% of its value overnight. Unemployment reached three million. A General Election was called for October 1931. The constituent parties of the National Government had not agreed a common programme, but asked for a 'doctor's mandate',

Edwin Gooch with Labour Party leader George Lansbury, NUAW rally at Folkingham, Lincolnshire c1935.

their propaganda raising the spectre of a total economic collapse under Labour.

Edwin Gooch stood for Parliament for the first time, up against the sitting Conservative member James Christie in South Norfolk. He addressed the electors: "The agricultural workers are practically voiceless in Parliament. I claim to know something of their conditions and should rejoice in the opportunity to speak for them... Ours is a religious crusade..." Despite this stirring sentiment he lost heavily. The election was a disaster nationally for Labour: they were down to just forty-six seats, back to their position in 1910.

Yet MacDonald's panic abandonment of his party had been futile. The Slump deepened. The hated Means Test was introduced for the "dole". Farmworkers, like many others, endured great privations in a time of terrible social division, with the Hunger Marches making very clear the sufferings of the unemployed.

Though the dominant theme of the polarised Thirties became the overt battle between Communism and Fascism, the Labour Party stuck to its democratic socialist guns, under first Lansbury then Clement Attlee. In 1931 the Communist Party had not won any seats, but neither had the New Party of the former Labour Chancellor of the Duchy of Lancaster, Oswald Mosley, already a quasi-Fascist. Instead the Labour Party methodically worked out a programme that could finally win them a working majority, one that would be practical and popular, strongly socialist in its tenets but also open to pluralism. In the countryside this would follow ideas laid out in their report *The Land and National Planning of Agriculture*.

Collective morale was gaining strength in the rural working class, and became the basis for regular public celebration, though Reg Groves in *Sharpen the Sickle* stresses that farmworkers still had to be discreet about their support for Labour. Union organisers often held open-air meetings to "invisible audiences" listening through cottage windows; General Secretary Bill Holmes wrote: "In many of our villages, a man who joins the trade union is worthy of the VC that's won on a battlefield... But to be a branch secretary! That is to risk one's livelihood every day of the week".

Edwin's son Michael Gooch remembered the NUAW gatherings of his youth as resembling county shows more than revolutionary insurrections. Every year there was the Fakenham Demonstration, the Mulbarton Rally and the Wymondham Great County Rally, usually with the New Buckenham Silver Band playing and the Union banners paraded. He was struck by the fact that it took six men to carry the great Norfolk county banner—two strong men with leather-sockets on their belts to hold the poles and four others hanging on to guy ropes. Hugh Dalton spoke at one Wymondham rally, as did the outspoken Hannen Swaffer of the *Daily Herald*. A poster urged "Come and Swell the Throng!", signed T.G.Higdon, County Secretary. A cyclostyled South Norfolk Labour Party song sheet [*England Arise! The long, long night is over* etc] from that time is preserved in the NUAW archive at the University of Reading.

Edwin's great-niece Pat Salmon remembered: "Michael and I used to go to Uncle Ted's Union meetings in the country, sometimes in the grounds of Quaker meeting houses where Michael and I would jump over the 'double-bed' tombstones—or in a field, where he would put up a stand and talk to a gathering..." Photographs show Edwin Gooch and other speakers perched rather precariously on hay waggons at gatherings in market places and village greens, the wheels wedged by half-bricks. Michael also had a memory of rolling along country lanes at election time in a Labour Party charabanc, red flags flying. His childhood autograph book, begun in the optimistic days of 1929, is a mix of family contributions and those of political figures: A.J.Cook, the left-wing leader of the miners in the General Strike, wrote "The Child of To-Day will be the Man of Tomorrow. Labour Has Won"; George Edwards added "Keep a smiling face all your days".

The farmworkers were supported by some interesting mavericks in those years, including various "red priests". Father McNab, a tonsured Dominican friar, had been a prominent figure during the Great Strike, addressing crowds of farmworkers in Fakenham market place. There were Christian Socialists (often High Church in their observances) such as the Rev. Conrad Noel at Thaxted, in Essex, who flew a red flag in church, and the Rev. George Chambers at Carbrooke, near Watton, where there was another annual Union meeting. Chambers was

The Red Priest: Edwin Gooch, George Lansbury, and an unknown Labour figure with Rev George Chambers, Vicar of Carbrooke.

notorious for commissioning a crucifix with Christ holding a hammer in one hand and a sickle in the other. Keelby in North Lincolnshire became the location for a regular Church Rally and in 1938, when Herbert Morrison MP was a special guest there, Edwin wrote of the accompanying "do" with relish: "We demolished piles of bread and butter and cakes in the Church Institute".

At the Fakenham Demonstration in August 1931 Edwin Gooch, seated on a farm waggon beside the elder statesman George Edwards, again pushed his ideal of consensus: "I want to see happiness and contentment in the countryside, and this can only come when the men are accepted as real partners in the industry".

In parallel with the workers' struggle for decent pay and conditions the farmers agitated for the abolition of Church of England tithes. The NUAW backed them in the long-running 'Tithe War' in principle, but with the proviso that their workers would benefit too. Edwin spoke at an anti-tithe event, and was blunt, stressing that it was a unique experience for him to be speaking at a meeting of farmers, and the first word he heard to the detriment of the labourers in regard to their wages and hours was the day he would walk out of the door and never return.

It would not come to that. But the tithe war was a side show. More important, as ever, was the struggle for fundamental rights. In January 1932 Edwin Gooch railed against the evils of the Means Test, and added an uncharacteristically bitter tirade against agricultural workers who had "voted against their own class" at the recent General Election. The Union was now campaigning for holidays with pay, the abolition of the tied cottage and power to the Central Wages Board to review county decisions. In December 1932 the press reported that "Mr E.G.Gooch, President of the NUAW, headed a deputation to the Minister of Labour yesterday to urge that unemployment insurance should be extended to agriculture"; a Royal Commission was considering the issue.

In 1932 Edwin was on the platform at Fakenham with George Lansbury, Labour's new leader, and Ben Tillett, legendary leader of the dockers—both regulars at NUAW events in the Thirties.

That winter saw a sudden crisis in Norfolk agriculture. The Executive of the Norfolk Farmers Union, having proposed a two shillings cut in wages, recommended that members dismiss as many men as possible as the Wages Committee had refused to let the rate drop below thirty shillings. By February 1933, with the NUAW standing firm, the crisis blew over and the 30/- wage apparently remained secure, but in May the NFU boycotted the Norfolk Wages Committee when they failed again to force the wage below that level.

At the same time as tackling this present-day crisis, the *Land Worker*, aware that tractors and other innovations were replacing horses—and consequently men—worried about the future in a 1933 article *Is The Machine a Menace?*: "... the machine, which should be a friend, is an enemy to us... none of us knows when these man-eating machines will take the bread off our tables". The issue gave urgency to the need to secure unemployment insurance for farmworkers.

The confidential details of the 1930 Agricultural Conference between the NUAW and NFU were revealed by the Union in the March 1933 *Land Worker*. The NUAW had pledged to campaign for higher wheat prices in exchange for the NFU stopping wage cuts. The Union claimed that the NFU had welched on the deal and therefore now felt obliged to "explain our conduct to our members". All plans for co-operation in the industry seemed to be off.

A Jolly Good Fore Horse

TRADE union and local and county council matters kept Edwin Gooch a very busy man. A 1933 *Land Worker* described the President's long day sitting on Forehoe Council dealing with the unemployed long after the chairman had left for home: "Bro. Gooch says he got home at 6.15pm and had the flu at 6.20pm!"

In the April 1933 issue *The President Keeps a Diary* described a typically busy month: "I have been glancing back in my engagement book and am astonished... I am quite certain I could not do it all, were it not for the sympathetic co-operation of my wife, who is also a county and district councillor, and does other public work. It means many lonely nights for her, I'm afraid".

There followed a list of a month's-worth of engagements, mostly in Norfolk—a mixture of committees and protest meetings that also included two visits to an old friend: "Called on the way and had a chat with our veteran leader, Sir George Edwards, who, I am delighted to say, is so much better in health"; and again three weeks later: "Saw Sir George at Fakenham. Found him still further improved. He will be campaigning with us again in the summer!" (George Edwards had been knighted in 1930.)

Edwin made one trip out of the county that month: "Off to London with Bros. Coe, Clarke, Harvey and the farmers' representatives, to interview the Minister of Agriculture with reference to the farming position in Norfolk. Our side put the men's case. We have 3,000 farm workers out of employment in this county. The farmers' spokesman supported our demand for insurance in the presence of the Minister. We felt that was worth going to London for."

He clarified: "I might add that I write on average six letters a day on Union and public work. There are always plenty of callers for advice, and I sign innumerable pension papers and other documents as a JP. I had almost forgotten to mention that I am not a full-time employee of the Union. My livelihood depends upon my attendance at an office in Norwich on most days of the week. And the rest is 'extras'!" He concluded on a wry "Norfolk" note: "It will be gathered that mine is a crowded but glorious life!"

Edwin's optimism about Sir George Edward's return to health was not justified for long. The revered founder and elder statesman of the Union died in December 1933, aged 83, and Edwin Gooch wrote a tribute in the *Land Worker*: "I regard it as one of the greatest pleasures and privileges of my life to have known

Edwin Gooch and George Lansbury enjoying a kerbside chat.

George Edwards". He mentioned George's autobiography *From Crow-Scaring to Westminster*, and revealed that he "passed it on to me to put it into shape, but I left it in his own simple language".

Looking back from 1937, Edwin wrote in memory of his kindred spirit: "George Edwards was a Methodist local preacher and the Sunday gatherings [of the Union] in the early days were after the style of the Methodist camp meetings. I recall the first such meeting I attended. We sang songs to hymn tunes; George read from the Bible and although he did not proceed along orthodox lines in the course of his address he did announce a text at the beginning". In a 1948 speech he recalled: "I knew George Edwards as a Methodist preacher whose religion was an everyday affair and who drew strength for his tasks from the Old Book".

Edwin Gooch had taken over Edwards' national role on the Central Wages Board and the Council for Agriculture, but instead of representing Norfolk in Parliament he was made an Alderman on Norfolk County Council, as was his wife Ethel from 1934. It was indeed a hectic life, with so many 'extras' on top of his regular job as chief sub-editor on the *Norwich Mercury*.

At the 1934 Biennial, Alderman G.E.Hewitt moved a vote of thanks: "I think we may well feel proud, especially we older men who have weathered the storm for years, when we see men like Bro.Gooch climbing the ladder of time behind us, because we know that this grand old Society will not go down when we do... When I was a young man, the waggons had only one pair of shafts and many

Cartoon by David Low commissioned by the TUC for its centenary book The Martyrs of Tolpuddle, *1934.*

a time I have been in the city of Norwich with four horses all in front of one another. When we have had a good fore horse we felt we were safe, because all the horses had to keep straight. I have always found Bro.Gooch a jolly good fore horse in our team".

Bro.T.G.Higdon of Burston seconded: "I am regarded personally as a rather left sort of chap. In respect of our President I can conscientiously and wholeheartedly say that he is as left as he is right, and as right as he is left. At the same time he is pretty well always right on the practical questions affecting the best interests of the Union. He is practical, and that is what we want. I am sure that so long as the interests of the Union are in his hands we shall be safe. Safety first, I think, has been the motto, unconsciously perhaps, of our chairman, and it may well be ours".

However, the policy of conciliation was not bearing fruit. The press reported the Presidential Address in May 1934: "Mr Gooch said 'The two years under review have been distinguished by attacks of all the agricultural wages committees on the economic position of the labourers. It has been a sorry chapter in the history of the farm worker. The period during which there was never so much state aid given to farmers has chosen further to depress the workers in the industry'."

That year, the centenary of the Tolpuddle Martyrs was marked with the carving of a headstone for James Hammett (the only one of the six who returned to his home) by Eric Gill, and the dedication of the TUC Memorial Cottages for NUAW veterans and their wives in the Dorset village. In the summer of 1935 the Union celebrated the 21st anniversary of the Burston School Strike with the Higdons, and Edwin was photographed on a waggon on the village green with Labour's leader George Lansbury, who had made a rousing speech ending with a plea for world peace; both are shown singing along with gusto to a solo violin.

The camaraderie of the Labour movement remained strong in adversity, and hopes were raised by Herbert Morrison's "sensational capture" of the London County Council in 1934. Other urban boroughs would follow. Then Lansbury, criticised for his pacifist stance as the threat of Fascism and Naziism grew, was replaced as leader by Clement Attlee. It seemed the party was a resurgent force, but Edwin Gooch's 1931 South Norfolk loss was repeated at the 1935 General Election, when Colin Clark was the Labour candidate. Though the party's parliamentary fortunes had improved considerably, the National Government, led by Stanley Baldwin, continued in power with a big majority. The scene was set for the appeasement of Hitler and Mussolini and all that followed.

Edwin Gooch's moderate philosophy of co-operation on condition of fair play was stressed in a speech he gave when elected President of the Norfolk Chamber of Agriculture in September 1935—a surprise to many, no doubt, but indicative of the respect he was earning across the industry: "In electing me to this office you have certainly overlooked much of my past and present record. For some years I have taken a very different line in the realm of agriculture, and as the Honorary President of the NUAW I have the interests of the farm workers as my first concern, and I shall continue to do so, but not to the exclusion of consideration of the wider interests of the industry. When I have felt that my services have been welcome I have not hesitated to offer them in the interests of the industry as a whole".

This was moderation in action, not a shift to the Right. In fact Edwin's stance and his political friends could come from almost anywhere on the socialist spectrum. Michael Gooch remembered, as an 11-year-old boy, being taken to a Union meeting in Walsingham while on holiday in Wells. His father had spotted the newly-weds Aneurin Bevan and Jennie Lee in the crowd and asked them up onto the platform to give impromptu speeches. They obliged. Edwin later wrote of this happy coincidence and these "brilliant and lovable comrades" in the *Land Worker*.

Edwin Gooch unveils the monument to Sir George Edwards, Fakenham Cemetery, 1935.

Edwin Gooch was elected to the National Executive Committee at the 1935 Labour Party Conference in Brighton, but did not seek re-election the following year due to pressure of other work.

In the autumn Edwin unveiled a granite memorial to Sir George Edwards in Fakenham Cemetery. Union members, ran part of the inscription: "...greatly valued his counsel and his delightful companionship throughout the years".

The *Land Worker* of November 1935 described:

"About a thousand people crowded round the graveside on that bright cold Sunday afternoon, and the deep silences, the singing of the hymns, the spoken words, were all of a moving quality.

Not a sad occasion. The crowd were gathered to hear the memorable words of the President, who spoke of that simple unveiling as 'to the glory of God and in memory of one best known as a friend to the poor'. It was the pence of the workers which had erected that stone, said Bro.Gooch. Granite was for steadfastness, that outstanding quality of one who stood firm to principle throughout his lifetime. Edwards had made a memorial for himself—the Union was that. But in years to come the farm workers would make pilgrimages to this sacred spot, and with bowed heads but with thankful hearts pay tribute to one of the greatest and most picturesque figures of English country history".

The *Land Worker* for January 1936 celebrated 'An Unemployment Insurance Bill at Last'. It was not perfect—agricultural workers would still receive less than those in other industries—but Reg Groves, writing *Sharpen the Sickle* in 1949, called his chapter on this period 'The Forward March'.

In June the NUAW journal reported on the Biennial Conference dinner:

"Bro.Gooch, from his place as chairman of proceedings, looked back over thirty years of Union growth. George Edwards's vision of 1906 had been realised. 'The farm workers have reaped huge advantages from the fact that we exist. Among those great advances won are the statutory minimum wage, the fixed hours of employment, holidays with pay, health and old age pensions, unemployment insurance, and representation in local and national government. Had the farm worker been silent, would all these changes for the better have been brought about?' Farm workers had looked doubtfully in the face of every one, and had said 'Oh, that'll never come'. But each had been won in turn, and every man who had loyally supported the Union had had some part in effecting these great changes for the better".

Hugh Dalton MP "an old friend of the farm workers" spoke last, stressing the gains made in rural constituencies at the last General Election: "Once we capture

Edwin and Ethel Gooch with NUAW delegates, 1930s. General Secretary Bill Holmes on left; former Organising Secretary James Lunnon on right.

the countryside you make a real Labour Government possible for the first time". His words were to be prophetic.

In November 1937 Edwin spoke in York on better homes for agricultural workers. Low wages in agriculture and attractive work elsewhere were leading to a drift from the land, he said, at a time when the land should be worked to its fullest capacity. (Within a couple of years both farmers and farmworkers would respond heroically to intense demands from the wartime government to increase productivity.) He was at Tolpuddle again in 1937, "Dr Dalton, my son Michael, and I", having sidetracked from a family holiday in North Wales.

Ethel remained Edwin's chief practical supporter and political comrade. In June 1938, shortly after an illness, he told the NUAW Biennial: "It has been a pleasure to serve this Movement. It has been a great privilege to me to meet you in the village and in your home. This is a real mighty, moving spiritual force which can carry all before it. A number of friends have made my work possible. May I mention one—my wife—without whose aid in many directions much of my work of the last two years would have been impossible, and without whose nursing in these recent days I should never have been fit enough to preside over this Conference [*loud applause*]". Edwin was re-elected President "with acclamation".

The Thirties had been a difficult decade for Labour, but the old Christian Socialist principles endured in a cruelly polarised world and these were ultimately years of achievement.

In E.G.Gooch's New Year message for 1939 printed in the *Land Worker* he quoted, in Primitive Methodist vein:

Help thou thy brother's boat across,
And lo, thine own has reached the shore.

Edwin Gooch caricatured in the Land Worker at the time of the 1945 Election victory.

On the Farm Front

DURING the Second World War the "farm front" was vital for a beleaguered nation's survival. Farmers and farmworkers in effect worked together to get the most out of a still largely unmechanised agriculture, though as described by John Stewart Collis in his celebrated account of working on farms as a volunteer, *The Worm Forgives The Plough*, relations between "master and man" were still distant and often strained. The Women's Land Army and prisoners of war supplemented the workforce. Edwin Gooch, for his part, did much for productivity by keeping relations between the National Union of Agricultural Workers and the National Farmers Union cordial. As early as May 1938 he had foreseen the crucial role of agriculture if war broke out, but also the impediments to any rapid or automatic increase in food production, in a speech to the Biennial Conference in London that was reported in the press:

> Mr E.G.Gooch in his presidential address urged the importance of agriculture in wartime, and said that so far, if war came, the part they should have to play in national defence would be "precisely nothing".

> "When is the Defence Minister to call together representatives of the farmers and farmworkers of this country in an endeavour to strengthen the weakest link in the chain of defence—the food link!" he asked.

> "It is not fair to lead people to believe that if war should come, all one has to do is to pass the word up to the farmyard and the cows, the hens, the bullocks, the sheep will at once proceed to do their best. You can't hurry nature.

> Even with possibilities of war, food production in this country is still restricted by order of Parliament.

> The fact of land going out of cultivation and thousands of men going off the land is viewed by many people with amazing complacency."

> Men left the land, he added, to get away from the deplorable housing conditions and they wanted at least 100,000 new additional cottages in the villages with modern conveniences.

In August 1938 he criticised Prime Minister Neville Chamberlain for blithely asserting that agricultural production would be adequate if war came.

Country life went on as normal through the Munich Crisis and in the looming shadow of war, though the wider world was a source of growing anxiety. The continuity of rural routines, as reported in the *Land Worker*, could seem rather unreal: in May 1939 Edwin was photographed at the Wheatacre Dinner, a teetotaller down the pub, captioned "The President Throws a Pretty Dart"; at the same time the NUAW journal was reporting the plight of Spanish refugees, and Jew-baiting in Nazi Germany.

Perhaps more unreal in Edwin's eyes was his invitation in July 1939 to an 'agricultural dinner' at Windsor Castle. It must have been quite a shock to get an envelope through the letterbox at *Rydal Mount* bearing the stamp of the Master of the Household. Having plucked up his courage he duly found himself seated at a glittering table opposite HM King George VI, between the Duke of Kent and the Earl of Athlone. In the *Land Worker* he later confided: "I am not as a rule very nervous, but I confess that the prospect of having to turn up at Windsor Castle in evening dress and meet such distinguished company caused me some concern. I am at home at branch dinners at village inns".

Just two months before the outbreak of war and the introduction of food rationing, the company had dined on, amongst many other dishes, *Turban de Sole Nantua*, *Salade Mimosa* and *Bombe Alhambra*. Members of the band of the Scots Guards entertained.

In covering the event the *Daily Express* profiled "blue-jowled, broad-shouldered Edwin Gooch". The news reached *The New York Times* a month later: "KING DINES LABOR CHIEF". Edwin was quoted: "During the dinner I reflected that at one time Dorsetshire farm workers were transported to Botany Bay for joining a trade union. Yet, just over 100 years later, I, as the leader of a farm workers union, was enjoying the hospitality of the King".

On returning to normality Bro.Gooch submitted an expenses claim to the Union for hire of clothes and a chauffeur.

Then on 17th August 1939 Tom Higdon died. Edwin, who would have known him well for at least twenty years, was at the crowded Burston Strike School for the memorial service, at which his widow Annie sang *Oh God Our Help in Ages Past*. Many present were in tears.

A fortnight later the Nazis invaded Poland, and on 3rd September Britain declared war.

In May 1940, with the Phoney War about to erupt into Blitzkrieg, another old friend and comrade died: George Lansbury, the former Labour Party leader, campaigning newspaper man and great pacifist who had met Hitler and Mussolini on peace missions in the late 1930s. He had hoped to the end "that

Wartime in Wymondham: standing from left Edwin and Ethel with Walter Lane, Walter Banham, Mabel Lane, Pip, Lucy and Pat Banham; seated: the widowed Sarah Banham, Freda Hayes, née Lane, with baby Kevin, born 1943, and his great-grandmother Ellen Lane. Seated below: Frances and Irene Mitchell, evacuees from Gravesend.

out of this terrible calamity will arise a spirit that will compel people to give up the reliance on force".

Edwin himself was clear that, king or commoner, everyone would need to make a united effort just to survive the war, let alone defeat the evil of Naziism. On 20th May 1940, when the British Expeditionary Force was reeling back across a shattered and chaotic land to Dunkirk, he spoke at Taunton on the need for a national effort in agriculture:

It is my opinion that the trade unions have done the proper thing in ranging themselves behind the war effort.

I believe this nation is up against the fight of its life—we are waging war today for life and liberty, and if the German hordes win this war, to put it mildly, we may never meet again in conference under the auspices of 'trade union'.

Alderman Gooch said that he considered that the Government must take complete control of agriculture and make every farmer and farmworker a civil servant.

As a trade union leader and member of the Labour Party, Edwin (and Ethel, too) would undoubtedly have been at personal risk if the Germans had invaded, though the couple's names were not in the "Black Book", the SS's notorious "Special Wanted List GB".

The National Union of Agricultural Workers' Head Office had been evacuated from London to Bushey, Herts, and as a wartime economy the *Land Worker* was printed as a news-sheet without covers.

In 1940 the Coalition Government, urged on by its formidable Minister of Labour Ernest Bevin, gave the Central Wages Board the power to boost morale (and productivity) in the countryside by setting a national minimum wage, a fundamental goal of the NUAW since 1921. The first offer was 42/-, but after a protest to Bevin by the Union it rose to 48/-.

Marginal 'waste' land was to be brought under cultivation, and Edwin urged that though "...Much land in Britain is still regarded as holy ground, and race-courses must on no account be ploughed up... There should not be a single acre of cultivable land left outside the scheme".

At the end of November 1940 Edwin Gooch was back on royal territory at Buckingham Palace, for an inspection by the King of the Trade Union Fleet of Mobile Canteens, to be handed over to the YMCA. NUAW members had donated one of them. A few days later this brand new machine was destroyed by bombing, but was quickly replaced.

Despite the travel restrictions and his local civil defence responsibilities in Wymondham, Edwin was still going around the country addressing meetings throughout the war. In February 1941 he wrote an article in the *Land Worker* entitled *The Union Spirit Fine Everywhere* about a hazardous trip north: "Bro. Hazell motored me to Doncaster from York, through the snow. We had to be dug out three times... Eventually reached home in time to hear the Midnight News. I had been on the road fifteen hours—just a day in the life of the President!"

Edwin Gooch became Vice-Chairman of both Norfolk Council Council and Norfolk Education Committee in 1941, when he was described by a political opponent as "an educationist in the best sense of the word". In Wymondham Edwin was put in charge of the town's wartime administration as Civil Co-ordinator and was Chairman of the Invasion Committee, issuing exhortations to not panic in the event of the Germans arriving on our shores. The townspeople were ordered to stay put and to do their bit. As he mentioned in a BBC radio talk in 1941 "my wife has cared for two [evacuees] since September 1939 and there will be tears on both sides when Frances and Irene Mitchell leave their Norfolk wartime home for Gravesend". The sisters, who had sailed to Great Yarmouth as part of a thousand-strong contingent of mothers and children on the day war broke out, would stay with Edwin and Ethel for almost the duration.

Ethel Gooch also had a very busy war in Norfolk and further afield. In January 1943 she was nominated by the Women's Cooperative Guild (part of the Cooperative Movement) to be a member of a sub-committee of the Ministry of Health's Central Housing Advisory Committee, convened in March 1942 and set up to consider the design of dwellings. The Labour-supporting Standing Joint Committee of Working Women's Organisations, or SJC, had lobbied for the sub-committee to be expanded to include "a representative of working class housewives", and Alderman Mrs E. G. Gooch JP and Cecily Cook—the General Secretary of the Guild—were added to their number. The WCG, SJC and other women's representative bodies contributed to the housing debate, through reports and questionnaires submitted to the Ministry of Health.

The sub-committee was chaired by the Earl of Dudley and included various professionals such as Louis de Soissons, the architect for Welwyn Garden City and three other architects (two of them female, including the Secretary Judith Ledeboer ARIBA), a doctor and a civil engineer; there was just one MP—Miss Megan Lloyd George—in their number, and several other figures from local government and the magistracy.

Design of Dwellings, published by HMSO in 1944, detailed the deficiencies of pre-war council housing, and devised national standards for new homes, increasing living space from 750 square feet (as determined by a 1923 Act) to 900 square feet. Facilities such as indoor bathrooms and lavatories were insisted upon. The Dudley Report set up a humane and well-considered template for post-war public housing in Britain's bombed cities. These homes remained spartan in many ways, without refrigerators or central heating, but by this single appointment Ethel Gooch and her fellow-committee members could be said to have contributed more to the country's well-being than almost anyone of their era.

The *Land Worker* reported on Ethel's various new posts in its February 1943 issue. As well as her national housing role she was Chairman of the Maternity and Child Welfare Committee on Norfolk County Council, a JP, President of the Women's Section of Wymondham Labour Party and President of the Women's Institute (her mother Sarah Banham was Vice-President, and niece Freda Lane was Hon. Secretary!). Ethel was also Centre Organiser of the Women's Voluntary Service, and had had two evacuees staying with her for over three years.

Perhaps it was a hopeful sign that the NUAW Biennial Conference was held in Bournemouth in the summer of 1942. Elsewhere, in speeches and articles Edwin Gooch urged on a record harvest in that critical year, when the U-boat campaign was threatening severe shortages. The press reported his words at

Norwich in July 1942: "A grave responsibility rests upon farmers and workers. We owe it as a duty to sons and brothers abroad and to Britain to put every ounce of energy we possess into the food production campaign. If Hitler wins there will be no wages but slavery and the concentration camp".

Edwin's and Ethel's attention would have been distracted from local and national business by air mail letters from abroad bringing news of their son Michael and his adventures in the Army. He had won a scholarship to Cambridge in 1941, and was allowed to do the first year of his architecture course on condition that he undertook (rather chaotic-sounding) officer training in the meantime. The call-up came in August 1942 and Michael Gooch joined the Royal Engineers; a year later, as a young lieutenant, he sailed in convoy for West Africa. In the Gold Coast (now Ghana) he trained Ashanti and Fanti sappers to form No.28 Works Company, West African Engineers. Just before D-Day they set off for India, passing through the Med and the Suez Canal before striking a rock in the Red Sea. After sitting there for two days, Michael, his men and about a thousand

Lt Michael Gooch of the Royal Engineers training Gold Coast sappers in Kumasi, in what is now Ghana, 1943.

others trans-shipped to a Dutch liner which was already packed with troops. They made it at last to Bombay.

In the wartime spirit of co-operation, rapprochement with the National Farmers Union was narrowly approved by delegates to the 1944 NUAW Biennial at Blackpool—with many cagey references to "leopards and spots, devils and long spoons"—but was not pursued much beyond cordial relations and positive gestures in the years to come. In fact, the NFU's President and Secretary had attended a meeting of the Union's Executive Committee just before the conference, so the process was already in train.

However, Edwin Gooch was under no illusion that his Union's membership remained under-rewarded for their efforts, as he stressed in a speech in March 1944 at the Farmers Club:

> In this war the nation has awakened to the fact that the farm workers are persons of such vast importance that we simply could not exist without them, yet an agricultural worker is still comparatively poorly paid: he is still poorly housed, he lacks water supply, sanitation, transport and educational facilities, diversions and entertainments—all of which are commonplace in the towns. We must face up to the fact that no agricultural policy that does not aim at providing every man on the farm with a minimum comparable to the wages in the towns will be enough to keep any but the old and the second-rate men on the land.

Edwin Gooch, profiled as "farmhand chief" by the press when appointed CBE in 1944.

Not long after presiding over the 1944 Biennial, Edwin Gooch was appointed CBE at Buckingham Palace for services to agriculture, and on 8th May 1945 (VE Day) he received a certificate from the Minister of Agriculture and Fisheries thanking him and the Norfolk War Agricultural Executive Committee for their contribution to the victory. They had "secured the willing co-operation of the farming community, and have, by their energy and example, raised the production of our farms, to a new high level".

By 1945 NUAW membership had soared to over 200,000—forming a powerful rural lobby—reversing the decline of the Thirties, and with the coming of peace a fresh start from a position of strength for agricultural workers seemed possible.

Noel-Buxton, sometime Liberal MP for North Norfolk, then Labour MP and Minister for Agriculture in Ramsay MacDonald's first government.

Labour Will Yet Capture the Countryside

EDWIN Gooch, aged fifty-six, was adopted as Labour's parliamentary candidate for the constituency of Northern (later North) Norfolk in February 1945 when an end to hostilities was at last coming in sight. He sensed the anticipatory national mood in an article for the *Land Worker*: "Mr Churchill makes a good war leader. I am not so certain about his qualifications as a peace leader".

On polling day that July the British public agreed with this reservation in vast numbers, and not only in the industrial towns and cities. Edwin Gooch was duly elected Member of Parliament, defeating the sitting Conservative MP Sir Thomas Cook with a huge swing of over 8,000 votes. Lt M.E.Gooch RE received the exciting news far away in India, a month or so before VJ-Day. He had sent in a postal vote from Chittagong, helping Chris Mayhew to take back South Norfolk for Labour. In fact all but one of the county's eight seats were won by the Labour Party—it was a local as well as a national landslide.

Until the 1931 election of Cook—a descendant of the founder of the travel firm, who lived in Edwardian splendour at Sennowe Park near Guist—the Northern Norfolk constituency, which had been the home territory of George Edwards, had had a long history of radicalism. Herbert Cozens-Hardy was its first Liberal MP in 1885, followed by William Gurdon at a by-election in 1899 caused by Cozens-Hardy's appointment as a High Court judge. His son William was the Cozens-Hardy who defeated Edwards in South Norfolk in 1918.

Noel Buxton, great-grandson of the abolitionist MP Thomas Fowell Buxton, was first elected for the Liberals in 1910, but lost the "Khaki Election" to Douglas King, an Independent Unionist. Buxton joined the Labour Party and won the seat back in 1922. The result was repeated in 1924, when Labour formed its first government, and Ramsay MacDonald made him Minister of Agriculture and Fisheries. Buxton was elevated to the Lords in 1930, as Baron Noel-Buxton of Aylsham, and his wife Lucy won the subsequent by-election. She lost heavily at the General Election of 1931 to Sir Thomas Cook, during the traumatic period of the National Government, and lost again in 1935 though his majority was halved.

Despite the difficult years of schism and National Government in the 1930s, Edwin Gooch had envisaged the possibility of Labour winning back rural seats at some future date in an Address to the 1936 Biennial: "Farm workers and their wives are less influenced today by a free tea, and gifts at Christmas, and by the risk of losing jobs and homes. They are voting for workers' candidates, and Labour will yet capture the countryside".

In the *Land Worker* of August 1945 he reflected on the Party's stunning victory. He had been reluctant to stand: "...although I was quite happy to carry on with my Union and public work, the friends were so insistent that I agreed to be the standard bearer". However "...it will be a great privilege to serve the people of my native county in Parliament. I represent a big stretch of country of real natural beauty and charm, and living there are a great number of humble folk who have been loyal to the Union and Party for very many years. I am glad of my success for their sakes. Their faith in the cause was fully justified." He thanked amongst many others his predecessors in the seat Lord and Lady Noel-Buxton for their practical assistance, and his wife who "was, as always, a very great help and the talks she gave at all my meetings were greatly appreciated by all the women".

He set out his stall for the period ahead: "Throughout the election I kept agriculture to the fore and I told farmers and workers that in the Labour Party's agriculture policy lay their salvation. Thus they know where I stand and in working to maintain an efficient and prosperous agriculture in North Norfolk I shall be working for the same throughout rural Britain. It will be my special pleasure to serve the farm workers and to endeavour to protect their interests and secure for them a place in the sun.

I am convinced there are five glorious years ahead for the people of this country and I'll try and play a man's part in the great tasks facing Britain."

On entering Parliament Edwin Gooch gave up his position as chief sub-editor for the *Norwich Mercury*, but continued as Honorary President of the National Union of Agricultural Workers, and this role informed a great many of his parliamentary contributions. In the NUJ's own newspaper, *The Journalist*, Edwin Gooch was profiled by Ernest Say of the *Daily Herald*: "E.G.Gooch is the 'Father' of our journalist MPs, and as the member for North Norfolk, his native county, has a record of public service probably unrivalled by any journalist in the country. His knowledge of agriculture, gathered in his work on his Norwich newspaper, where he worked for many years as a sub-editor, aroused in his sensitive character a keen interest in the conditions of the men who toil on the land. He has been for years a member of our Union and determined to help their organisation. He is indeed a human dynamo..."

Labour's success was celebrated in frisky style by an NUAW dinner in Holborn, with Herbert Morrison MP again a guest and ventriloqual entertainment by "C.Campkin and his Doll", plus "Fun & Frolic" on the piano. Morrison, now Deputy Prime Minister, returned to address the Union's annual dinner in London in October: "...there is a breath of fresh country air in the new House of Commons. At last the vote of the agricultural community is no longer the monopoly of one party. There have been earth tremors among previously 'safe' Tory rural seats. Norfolk, Suffolk, Essex, Cambridgeshire sent back a team of Labour MPs. Your president, Edwin Gooch, turned a Tory majority of over 3,000 into a Labour victory with a Labour majority of over 5,000 in the division of Northern Norfolk."

Hansard, recording every word spoken in the Commons, is now available online; so it is possible to trace Edwin's interventions, large and small, down the years, and to imagine his broad Norfolk accent deployed in the 'Mother of Parliaments'.

After asking various questions of ministers that autumn, on issues such as sea defences and the dismissal of farmworkers and their replacement by low-cost German prisoners of war, Edwin Gooch MP made his maiden speech in the House of Commons on December 20th 1945. Contributing to a debate on land resettlement, in particular the allocation of smallholdings, he included a personal note: "I live in the country. I am one of those men who can see beauty in a country lane in December. I love works of art, but to me there is nothing so beautiful as the natural art of the countryside".

In October 1945 Edwin had made his first foreign trip, crossing the Atlantic on the *Queen Mary*, which was taking 11,000 GIs home. He went as an adviser— as did Sir James Turner, President of the NFU—and part of the 30-strong UK Delegation to the United Nations' founding First Session of the Food and Agricultural Organisation. This conference, held in Quebec, marked, now that the war was won, the permanent creation of a body for both health and agriculture dedicated to the ending of malnutrition worldwide. Sir John Boyd-Orr, the celebrated nutritionist, had been elected the first Director General of FAO at the preparatory meeting in Hot Springs, Virginia, two years earlier, convened by President Roosevelt.

In April 1946 Edwin Gooch was present at the London congress that revived the International Landworkers' Federation, established in the 1920s by agricultural trade unions. Edwin chaired a dinner for the ILF at the House of Lords at which Bro.Gooch welcomed the delegates: "Here we are free to meet as trade unionists, and it is appropriate that London should be the first post-war meeting place... despite the pounding we had this country remained the land of the free". His son Michael, very recently returned from serving with the Royal

Engineers in India, demobbed and about to resume his interrupted studies at Cambridge, was present at the feast. The *Land Worker* reported: "Some of the delegates who had known the rigours of German Occupation said they had not had a meal like it in six years".

Edwin Gooch was elected to the Labour Party National Executive Committee in June 1946, ten years after he first served, and would remain a member for the next fifteen years.

In October 1946 Edwin was at the follow-up Second Session of the FAO, a conference held in Copenhagen, as the only union leader there, and heard New York Mayor Fiorello la Guardia, Director-General of UNRRA, the agency for refugees, describe the new organisation as "the hope of the world".

Despite many new commitments as an MP it was Edwin's long-standing role as NUAW President that still informed his broader political activity. The 1946 Biennial Conference was hailed in the *Land Worker* for June as "probably the best ever", evidence of a progressive spirit among the rural workforce: "Here was nothing to remind one of the ideal old-world rustic, so charmingly deferential in his smock, whose talk was limited to the weather and the condition of cows, and who was content to be regarded as the cart-horse of society—a lowly position allocated to him by Divine Providence. A more alert-looking lot of men than the delegates it would have been difficult to find—genuine 'sons of the soil' filled with fervour springing from the consciousness of the justice of their aims and of the determination to achieve them."

That workforce was being undermined in various ways by unpaid labour, as a hangover from wartime. In a speech at Bedford in October 1946 Edwin Gooch MP declared: "We have got the queerest collection on the farms that I can ever remember... Italian and German PoWs, Polish soldiers, conscientious objectors, women of the Land Army, and children who ought to be at school. When are we going back to the policy of British workers for British farms?" The issue of prisoners of war keeping native workers out of jobs rumbled on, with Edwin fulminating in November 1947: "A good British farmworker is worth four Germans on the farms of Britain".

Over the years he made a succession of speeches and interventions in the Commons on the theme of the abolition of the tied cottage, the first being in February 1946, when he noted that farmers were repossessing properties to create tied accommodation in place of standard tenancies. The issue arose again in October 1946 as part of the debate on the Hill Farming Bill: "It has been said again and again that the Englishman's home is his castle. I think we must add to that 'except in rural England'." It would be a long battle for the NUAW. In January 1947 the *Land Worker* published photographs of evictions; in April that year Edwin, speaking in Parliament, compared the security gained for urban dwellers by Rent Restriction Acts with the ever-present risk of eviction from a tied cottage; in April 1948 more evictions were reported by the Union's journal under the headline *Man's Inhumanity to Man.*

At the 1949 Labour Party Conference in Blackpool, Nye Bevan, Minister of Health, assured delegates that in the next Parliament there would be "reconsideration of the position of the tied cottages, an institution which contains many features repugnant to the Labour movement. The unions will be consulted as to the best means of removing these features and giving the farm workers the measure of security in their homes enjoyed by other workers". This promise depended on a second Labour victory.

Farmworkers' minimum wages had been protected during the war, but now the farmers were less willing to comply. In a debate on Agricultural Policy on 25th February 1946, Edwin Gooch MP complained that farmers' representatives on the Central Wages Board had voted against a 48-hour week, six bank holidays with pay, and an increase in overtime rates. He read out a letter from a farmworker's wife struggling to survive on £3 10s 0d a week, and questioned the whole concept of grading based on an inadequate minimum wage.

He raised the spectre of strikes in the countryside: "I should be very sorry if this fine body of men, a most loyal body of workers who never lost a day from the farms during the war, were compelled to come out on strike during the lifetime of a Labour government in order to get their just due."

Such desperate action was not necessary. In November 1946 the House was debating the Agricultural Wages (Regulation) Bill, a precursor to Labour's promised full programme of support for agriculture, and Edwin Gooch spoke on the importance of a national Agricultural Wages Board to replace the much-abused local county committees:

"I personally welcome this Bill, and I am sure that welcome is shared by all the farm workers in this country. It has long been apparent to most people that the Government means business with regard to the nation's greatest single industry. The Labour Party is no longer purely an industrial party; many of us have been sent here by the votes of farmers and farm workers on the strength of the party's promises, and I am sure the Government will not let down either farmers or workers. The farming community, I am glad to say, can no longer be regarded as one of the hind-wheels of the Tory chariot.

By making permanent wage-fixing machinery in agriculture, the Government will enable farm workers to consolidate their position. I hope there will be no going back in the matter of wages. Not only can the farmers as a body plan ahead with confidence, knowing that under a Labour Government they will be safeguarded, but the farm workers, whose labours are so vital to the nation at this stage, can go forward to play their part in peace as in war, knowing that they will receive a just reward for their labours."

He went on to describe the struggle of the Norfolk farmworkers in 1923, in the face of a wages free-for-all. Improved wages were essential post-war, but these were still the years of austerity. Extra food rations were available for men who worked on the land, but farmers were not applying on their behalf. Edwin urged that men, or their wives, should be allowed to apply for "a bit more meat" themselves.

A *Land Worker* editorial of December 1946 was headlined "THE UNION'S GREATEST YEAR" and was a panegyric to the good life under Labour: "The story of the Union is at once a record of enormous gains for the workers and a romance. A new country life has been born. Minimum wages are now fixed by law. The earnings of farmworkers are now comparable with those of many other workers... It is mainly due to the efforts of the Union that the land worker is now treated not as a serf, but as a citizen".

In September 1947 Edwin attended the Permanent Agricultural Committee of the United Nations International Labour Office in Geneva, and he would be made Chairman of the ILO in 1949. Founded in 1919 the ILO was something of lasting value that had been created by the Treaty of Versailles, inspired by ideals of social justice and the creation of humane conditions for workers.

Edwin wrote in the *Land Worker* on his return from Geneva: "To attend three International Conferences in three years was not only totally unexpected, but was an entirely new activity for a stay-at-home like myself". These were still very difficult times in Europe, with the Marshall Plan not yet in operation, and Edwin noted both the lack of food on the train from Paris and the wealth of neutral Switzerland. In November 1947 he reported for the journal on a very different and timeless gathering at Brent Eleigh, in Suffolk, in *At The Harvest Horkey*.

Edwin Gooch's advocacy of government protection for both farming and farm workers was influential at the Standing Committee stage of the Labour Government's Agriculture Wages (Regulation) Act, 1947—a measure which he described as "revolutionary"—that established the regulatory machinery that remained in operation until recent years in England and continues in Scotland and Wales.

He had attempted to increase workers' representation on the wages board from two to three—equal numbers with the farmers and landlords—but had been defeated (*President's Fight for Countryside Equity*, headlined the *Land Worker*). He recalled that this had been made Labour Party policy as far back as 1926, and criticised the Minister of Agriculture, Tom Williams, for not putting it into practise now.

In 1947, as part of the annual Tolpuddle celebrations, in company with the Union's old friend Hugh Dalton, now Chancellor of the Exchequer, Edwin Gooch MP, President of the NUAW, unveiled a bronze plaque on the façade of the Old Assize Courts in Dorchester, from whence the Martyrs had been transported to Botany Bay.

There was much to celebrate in 1947. As well as wage regulation, one of Labour's great achievements was the Agriculture Act, creating an assured market and guaranteed prices. Tom Williams declared it would "promote a healthy and efficient agriculture capable of producing that part of the nation's food which is required from home sources at the lowest prices consistent with the provision of adequate remuneration and decent living conditions for farmers and workers, with a reasonable return on capital invested". It was the spirit of sweet reasonableness in action, and created something of a golden age for British farming.

In 1948 Edwin was in Denmark for a Summer School organised by the Workers' Educational Association and reported: "Danish newspapers recorded all our movements and one ventured to describe me as 'a mild type of Socialist'. I didn't know whether to take that as a compliment or not!"

Hugh Dalton MP, Chancellor of the Exchequer, guest of honour of the NUAW at the 1947 Tolpuddle Rally.

Plaque commemorating the Tolpuddle Martyrs on Dorchester Shire Hall, unveiled by Edwin Gooch MP in July 1947.

He travelled in style on his second trip to North America in November 1948 as an adviser to the British delegation attending the Fourth Session of the UN's Food and Agriculture Organisation. Edwin's report for the *Land Worker* in early 1949 is agog at the wealth of the post-war USA. He had sailed on the luxurious

Mauretania and as an inveterate smoker had been delighted to find twenty *Gold Flake* cigarettes cost just a shilling, duty-free, on board. An *On the Waterfront*-style longshoremen's strike in New York had meant the liner had been diverted to Halifax, Nova Scotia, but Edwin Gooch and fourteen others were flown by the Canadian Air Force to New York, then on by train to Washington and the FAO Conference. Though his terminology is now very dated and far from PC, Edwin was sympathetic to the "coloured attendants" on the trains. He "liked the look of the coal-black mammies, in their white dresses" serving in restaurants. Segregation, he thought, was not apparent in the workplace. He met President Harry S Truman

Ernest Bevin, Foreign Secretary, greeted by Edwin Gooch on his 1948 visit to Wymondham to make a speech at the Regent Cinema, filmed by Pathé News.

and enjoyed a Thanksgiving dinner. His voyage home to Liverpool was from Montreal on the *Empress of Canada*.

Perhaps as a result of Edwin's new international role, Foreign Secretary Ernest Bevin chose to come to Wymondham in 1948 to make a speech about the current state of Europe, the Marshall Plan, and the need to bring Germany back into the democratic fold. Pathé News filmed the formidable figure of Bevin holding forth on a stage at the town's Regent Cinema, with Edwin Gooch MP sitting beside him.

All this high table business could have gone to Edwin's head, but his feet were always very firmly on the ground. Back in Parliament in March 1949 he raised the issue of children being taken out of school to help with the harvest. He repeatedly brought up the urgent issue of protecting farmworkers against insecticide spray—five had died by November 1950.

He remained very aware of the Union's debt to its pioneers and to past struggles. In April 1949 Edwin Gooch spoke in tribute to his old friend George Hewitt, the hero of the 1911 St Faith's Strike, who had died. On May Day that year Prime Minister Clement Attlee (who had spoken at an NUAW rally in Skegness the year before) joined Edwin in laying wreaths on the grave of Sir George Edwards at Fakenham; and shortly afterwards Edwin initiated an annual

Union rally at Wellesbourne, near the Warwickshire home of the farmworkers' first champion Joseph Arch. The press reported six hundred farmworkers gathered "round the stump of an old chestnut tree" under which Arch had founded the pioneering National Agricultural Labourers' Union; in his speech Mr E.G.Gooch MP declared that the "prosperity and conditions of the workers compared with those of Arch's day constituted a complete revolution".

At a 5,000-strong NUAW gathering in Great Yarmouth in July 1949, Home Secretary Herbert Morrison was once more the chief guest, and he and Edwin were photographed seated in a rowing boat mounted on a trailer and drawn along Marine Parade by Union men, in a sort of comic version of an imperial progress. At the rally Edwin urged members: "Don't kid yourselves that 1923 cannot be repeated. With a Tory Government it would be". Morrison outlined all the benefits that Labour had brought in: the National Health Service, National Insurance, rural housing, the improved supply of electricity to farms and villages, the provision of mains water and sewerage—a revolution had taken place in the countryside and trade unionism and the Labour Party had achieved it. He concluded: "We've got the right Government—the first to treat you properly for 150 long and tragic years. Keep it!"

Under a Labour Government the old battles for basic rights seemed to be part of history; the Left's political objectives had been achieved with the creation of the Welfare State, the National Health Service and the nationalisation of key industries like the railways, steel and coal. There was, nevertheless, in a period when the USSR was still riding high in public esteem after the Red Army's great wartime sacrifices, a vexed issue of how far to the left Labour should go.

Churchill had made his famous 'Iron Curtain' speech in March 1946 and at that summer's NUAW Biennial Conference there had been quite a row, as the *Land Worker* revealed: "The smashing defeat of a resolution advocating a Communist affiliation to the Labour Party was a foregone conclusion. There were some

---

NATIONAL UNION OF AGRICULTURAL WORKERS

HEAR—TOM BRADDOCK, M.P.
E. G. GOOCH, M.P., *President N.U.A.W.*
A. C. DANN, *General Secretary*
FRED BROWN, *Executive Committee*
A. E. JORDAN, *Dorset Organiser*
at the

Working Class Event of 1949

THE ANNUAL TRADE UNION PROCESSION & DEMONSTRATION
on Sunday, July 17th at 4 p.m. in

TOLPUDDLE

PROGRAMME
Morning   Visit places of interest
1 p.m.   Music on the lawn
2.30 p.m. 1st performance of play
4 p.m.   Procession
4.30 p.m. Meeting addressed by 2 M.P.'s
          Tea interval
6.30 p.m. 2nd performance of play
6.30 p.m. Trade Union Meeting
9 p.m.   Finish

Catering for 4000 from Noon onwards

Don't miss this! Book your coach now
Printed by the Wright Printing Co., Blandford—1875. T.U. Telephone 178   P.T.O.

Programme for the 1949 Tolpuddle Procession and Demonstration, which saw a confrontation with members of the Communist Party.

forthright speeches in which the humbug of smooth words, too often tinged with insincerity, was discarded. The President's statement, admirable in spirit and temper, was unanswerable. Farm workers, in common with the great majority of other workers, favour the British way to Socialism, and will do nothing to push our country down the slippery slope to totalitarianism". A similar move was heavily defeated at the 1946 Labour Party Conference.

Two years later the notionally democratic Czechoslovakia had been transformed into a one-party state with a constitution confirming the "leading role" of the Communist Party and the dictatorship of the proletariat. The Cold War had, in effect, begun.

In the summer of 1949 a large group of communists tried to join the annual Tolpuddle Procession, prompting several NUAW branches plus Edwin Gooch, President, and Alf Dann, General Secretary, to quit the march in protest. In the Land Worker Edwin explained his position: "I came down in all good faith to honour the memory of the Tolpuddle Martyrs and not to take part in a Communist parade... I have no use for the hammer and sickle, an emblem of a political creed which is foreign to our people. The Union Jack under a Labour Government is good enough for me. The basis of our creed is Social Democracy, and Fascism and Communism are foreign to it. The Martyrs... took the stand for freedom. Communism is the very negation of freedom and liberty, and should have no part in the trade union movement".

He later expressed doubts about one Labour tenet, in response to criticism from the Communist rural paper County Standard: "Nationalisation of the land or of farming would not of itself produce more food". The generally poor performance of Soviet collective farms would bear this out.

Edwin was clearly a Centre-Left pragmatist rather than a dogmatist of Right or Left, but nevertheless he was not one to bear a grudge indefinitely, as Wilf Page, his agent in North Norfolk testified; after the openly Marxist Page quit in 1949 in protest against Labour policies, Edwin did not speak to him for two years (perhaps out of disappointment in the loss of his larger-than-life protégé and potential successor in the Union), but then they met in the street and Wilf praised Edwin's strong stance against German rearmament and so their friendship was resumed.

Edwin Gooch, President, and Alf Dann, General Secretary of the NUAW from 1945.

Despite political differences Edwin Gooch got on very well with his agent in North Norfolk, Wilf Page, a card-carrying Communist.

1945   GOOCH
1950   **GOOCH**
1951   GOOCH
1955? Well, why not?

The

Election Address

To ensure continuity of service
by a Norfolk man in the interests
of Norfolk people, without regard
to party, class or creed

Again Vote

GOOCH

The Returning Officer will send you
a Poll Card with your Register Number
and the Polling place at which you vote.

of

Ald. E. G. Gooch,

C.B.E., J.P.

Polling Day:

Thursday,   May   26th

7 a.m. to 9 p.m.

No one need know how you vote
but yourself!

1955 General Election flyer for North Norfolk. Edwin Gooch — well, why not?

Even Tory MPs have Consciences

EDWIN Gooch was re-elected for North Norfolk in 1950, but the Labour Government's majority was down to five. Speaking at that year's National Union of Agricultural Workers' Biennial in Margate, the President cautioned: "The Labour Government has quite properly taken office: for how long remains to be seen... I imagine the Tories will again be up to their tricks". In 1951 the Union secured two weeks' paid holiday for its members, but not the promised abolition of the tied cottage. There was no time for more reforms. In such a precarious situation another contest was inevitable, and Clement Attlee called a snap General Election in October 1951. The gamble almost succeeded, as Labour gained most votes overall, but due to the eccentricities of the first-past-the-post system they lost to Winston Churchill's Conservatives, who emerged with a seventeen seat majority. Despite the loss of three Norfolk seats to the Tories, Edwin Gooch was re-elected for North Norfolk that year.

What were the implications for farmworkers of a Conservative Government? There was anxiety that the Tories would backslide on the fair terms and mechanisms established by the 1947 Agriculture Act, but Edwin's answer was a positive one: to pursue his vision of the industry as an economic whole, with farmers and workers interdependent.

Food shortages remained a problem and the nation was still subject to rationing. The system would not finally be wound up until 1954, nine years after the end of the war, when meat was the last staple to come off the ration. Some were keen to find scapegoats in farmers themselves, but Edwin Gooch, North Norfolk, stressed their virtues in reply to an attack from his own side on the farmers in the House in April 1952:

"I wish he [Hon. Member for Wednesbury, S.N.Evans, Lab] would occasionally give his mind to dealing with what, after all, is the very critical food situation that faces us at the present time. The line he takes today, and has always taken, is a temptation to me; but slanging farmers in the bunch will not take us anywhere. I know, because I have been doing a bit of that these last thirty-five years when I thought the farmer needed it, and I am prepared to do a bit more when the circumstances warrant it, but we are all in this business of food production together, and if some people are making fortunes out of food, we can devise ways and means of putting the brake on without setting up a Royal Commission.

At the same time as we are attending to the man who is making a fortune out of food production, I think we should give a thought to the thousands of small farmers who are still the backbone of British agriculture, and the thousands of farmworkers, the most patient of men, whose sole desire is to give of their best in return for a fair reward. I wish to place on record today the fact that there has not been a strike in British agriculture for thirty years".

But the battle to improve the farmworkers' lot was not forgotten. In June 1952, in a parliamentary debate on the drive for greater food production, Edwin reported on the visit of some Australian delegates to Norfolk who had expressed surprise at the cheapness of agricultural labour, at half the Australian rate. The *Land Worker* printed Ministry of Agriculture figures for fatal accidents on farms in England and Wales for the four years from 1949 to 1952, totalling 487—the largest proportion of which were due to machinery, but also falls from stacks and ricks, gunshots, bulls and other animals, electrocution and lightning.

The struggle to end the tied cottage continued. Edwin declared this anachronism, using some Biblical phraseology, as "...socially and morally wrong. They tie a man hand and foot... The party opposite want to perpetuate the tied

Edwin Gooch addresses a brick, Sheringham 1952: constructing a field stove as part of a civil defence exercise, watched by Dr Lincoln Ralphs, left, Norfolk's Chief Education Officer.

cottage system, but I made a remarkable discovery during the debates on the Housing Bill, and that is that even Tory MPs have consciences, and even some National Liberals have consciences. Their consciences must have smote them on this occasion and made them wonder whether they should allow the law to continue or whether they should give four weeks' grace to an occupant of a tied cottage before he is turned out".

Around this time Michael Gooch met his future wife Sheila Ward while both were working as architects in the London County Council's vast, 1,000-strong Architects' Department in County Hall, designing new schools for the Blitzed capital. They would occasionally pop over Westminster Bridge to the House of Commons to meet Edwin for lunch.

Sheila remembered travelling up to Wymondham for the first time (as a Londoner she had no idea where she was going, being not quite sure where Norfolk was) and causing a local sensation by wearing slacks. She thought she had annoyed her hosts—proud of their ancient town—by talking of "going down the village". She had to adapt quickly to no-frills rural ways, taking on the challenge of Ethel's "massive teas, meat pies... a bowl of raspberries wriggling with little worms. I went 'Eurggh!', but Edwin wolfed them down, saying 'Extra nourishment!'" Michael proposed to Sheila in the garden at *Rydal Mount* and they married in May 1952 in Wimbledon.

Unfortunately this happy turn of events soon became the hardest of times for Edwin Gooch. His resolve in sustaining such a busy public life was challenged to the utmost when his wife Ethel died suddenly on 6th February 1953 in Wymondham, aged sixty-four, ending what was very much a political team as well as an enduring marriage. It was a huge loss, both private and public, as is made clear by the many tributes to her sterling qualities.

The *Land Worker* printed an obituary:

"For many years—right up to the week of her death—Mrs Gooch had brought to a wide range of social duties the rare gifts of mind and character with which she was endowed.

Throughout her life Mrs Gooch brought to the administration of social affairs a clear, logical and practical mind, a courageous intellectual honesty, and a great tolerance of spirit, based upon her

Possibly the last photograph taken of Edwin and Ethel Gooch together before her sudden death in 1953.

Ethel Gooch presents a silver NUAW badge, watched by Edwin and Albert Hilton of the NUAW, future MP for South-West Norfolk.

wide and sympathetic understanding of life itself. Her great contribution to the social welfare of her town and county will be grievously missed. The loss of his wife is a terrible blow to Bro.Gooch, who ever found her a willing and devoted helpmeet and a most efficient helper in all his good works.

...all were united in mourning the loss of one who so sincerely committed herself to the understanding and remedying of social problems with such intelligence and kindliness."

The *Norfolk Chronicle*, reporting on a very public funeral, listed Mrs E. G. Gooch's many roles, locally as County Alderman and long-standing member of Norfolk Education Committee, magistrate, ex-chairman of Wymondham UDC (in 1951), and nationally as a member of the Central Housing Advisory Committee.

The funeral in Wymondham was a great gathering of representatives of all the many official bodies Ethel had been involved with over the years, including Morgan Phillips, General Secretary of the Labour Party, and other Labour figures. Sam Peel, Chairman of the Norfolk Education Committee, was there with other County Councillors, and colleagues from various local schools, the Women's Institute and the National Union of Agricultural Workers. The newspaper listed about 200 names, and hinted at many more attending. Among the floral tributes was one from Edwin Gooch's defeated opponent in North Norfolk in 1945, Sir Thomas Cook.

Captain Denny, a Wymondham Magistrate, later gave a tribute: "[Mrs Gooch] had what were perhaps the two most important attributes for making a good magistrate. One was a great knowledge of and sympathy with her fellow men, and the other a balanced and judicial mind. She would be greatly missed."

This was not simply a public loss. Leafing through a well-thumbed copy of *The Oxford Book of English Verse*, an edition from 1906 with the name Ethel Banham inscribed on the fly leaf, I found tucked into the back Shakespeare's mournful *The Phœnix and The Turtle*, typed on House of Commons headed notepaper. The theme of the poem is how two lovers—in this case two birds, the female phoenix and the male turtledove—can be one, in defiance of reason and of the grave:

> *So they loved, as love in twain*
> *Had the essence but in one;*
> *Two distincts, division none:*
> *Number there in love was slain.*

I don't know whether the poem was intended to be read at the funeral, which in the 1950s was not the usual mode, but the words of the Bard must have consoled Edwin a little as he mourned the loss of his soul-mate.

Shortly before Ethel's death, Alf Dann the NUAW General Secretary had died, and a year earlier James Lunnon, the Union pioneer. Dann was replaced as General Secretary by Harold Collison.

A week before Edwin's life was turned upside down, a vast natural disaster had engulfed the East Coast, including much of his constituency. One hundred people drowned in Norfolk alone in the sea surge on the night of the 31st January 1953.

The impression given from *Hansard* in the preceding years is of some inertia regarding coastal protection. As early as November 1945 Edwin Gooch, North Norfolk, had asked questions of the Minister (Aneurin Bevan) about sea defences being made a national rather than local charge. In May 1946 he asked Herbert Morrison MP, the Deputy Prime Minister, who was due to visit Norfolk to make a speech, about coastal erosion; would he "...spare a little time to look at the colossal problem with which that county is faced?" Morrison replied, perhaps with a sigh: "I will think about it, but I was hoping to have a little rest when I was not on the platform".

As soon as he was able, Edwin came down to London and spoke in the Commons about the floods, on 19th February 1953:

"Perhaps I may add that domestic tragedy in my home prevented me from being as active as I wanted to be in the stricken parts of my constituency. On the Sunday following the disaster, however, I travelled many miles through the badly-hit part of the North Norfolk constituency, and all I can say about what I saw that day is that the scenes were almost indescribable. I add my word to those who have spoken from this side of the House in saying that it is not my intention to approach this matter from a party standpoint. In North Norfolk we are one people in desiring to see the damage repaired and steps taken to prevent a recurrence of the disaster if humanly possible."

In the aftermath of his great personal loss *Rydal Mount* was kept going by a succession of housekeepers, but for the rest of the decade Edwin Gooch would live alone. Perhaps as a result he threw himself into local, national and international political activity more than ever. His daughter-in-law Sheila accompanied him to a Buckingham Palace garden party and sat with him on a grandstand erected within the Palace of Westminster to watch the Coronation of Queen Elizabeth II. Michael and Sheila moved out of London in 1954 and after a couple of years in Northampton were living nearby in Norwich, busy with their architectural work in the city and bringing up their children Simon and Joanna.

As he had done twenty years earlier, Michael assisted his father on campaign in 1959, touring the back lanes of the constituency with him in a loudspeaker van, flying the red flag.

International Landworkers

DESPITE the long years spent in Opposition by the Labour Party in the 1950s, for the President of the National Union of Agricultural Workers it was business as usual locally, nationally and especially abroad, starting with a trip to Paris in September 1951 to attend the 9th World Poultry Congress, about which he wrote in wry vein in the *Land Worker*: "I never thought that the humble hen and what it produces would provide material not only for discussions by two international organisations but also sufficient problems to provide an agenda for a week's conference... It did not occur to me that the hen might prove a factor in determining world peace...". He was less than impressed with an unromantic post-war Paris, which "needed a coat of paint and a bit of Spring cleaning".

Shortly afterwards he was in Sweden with a Labour Party delegation as guests of the Social Democrats and their "great and lovable" long-serving Prime Minister Tage Erlander, enjoying a trip to the "frozen North", where it was unseasonably hot, forcing Edwin (for once) to remove his jacket. He was pictured with some picturesque Lapps—Sami, as we would now say—in national costume, and admiring their dried stockfish.

Welcome to Lapland: Edwin Gooch MP travelled to Sweden as guest of the Social Democrat government.

He was in Salzburg and Hamburg for the International Landworkers Federation in 1952, and Geneva for the International Labour Organisation in 1953. On one of these trips, according to family legend, Edwin used an old-fashioned and lethal-sounding paternoster lift in a hotel and was carried on up to the top of the slow-moving non-stop belt of platforms, over the winding mechanism and back down the far side!

Adrian de Ruyter, seated at right, was General Secretary of the European Landworkers Federation for the ten years Edwin Gooch was President of the ILF from 1950.

Closer to home, in a speech at Brighton, Edwin defended subsidies to farmers as they sustained a wage-rise for farm workers: "Talk of feather-bedded farmers gets the headlines. Why not come along and help to feather-bed the men who keep the industry going and who have been sleeping on a hard plank for so long?"

In another speech in the winter of 1953/4 at the annual dinner of the Downham Market District Committee in Norfolk, Bro.Gooch laid out his co-operative approach to rural affairs:

Edwin Gooch, President of the ILF, speaking at a rally in Italy.

"I sometimes think it is unfortunate that farmers and workers operate in separate compartments when dealing with the welfare of farming. If disaster comes to farming we all go down the drain together. It was so last time. Why cannot we do a bit of collective thinking? Why cannot we envisage working together on policy?

Edwin Gooch in Switzerland with ILF delegates from Kenya and Suffolk.

The change from controls to a freer economy has caused an upheaval of the first magnitude, and I ask myself, is history to repeat itself? I am not happy about the undermining of the Agriculture Act and the substitution of the present makeshift policy.

...I subscribe to the idea that farming should be regarded as a public service. Its contribution to national health and welfare can be, and is, enormous, and at the same time it can help the old country over its economic difficulties. The people engaged in it are entitled to a good livelihood, security, and a feeling of confidence."

The 1954 Biennial marked Edwin's silver jubilee as President. He had seen the National Union of Agricultural Workers grow "from a small and struggling organisation with only £32,000 in the bank, to a thriving national movement with funds of £444,000." The *Land Worker* sketched his early career from his father's blacksmith's forge, to printer's compositor and journalist, then his election to parish, rural and county councils and the magistracy—all in a rush in 1922.

Edwin had ruminated on the milestone in an article, *Retrospect and Resolve,* in May 1954:

"I was sitting in a tea car journeying through France on the way to an international meeting in Geneva when a friend asked me how long I had been President of the NUAW. I consulted my diary and discovered that I was first appointed in 1928.

'That's 25 years ago,' remarked my friend. And so it was at the time we were talking."

He went on to reminisce about the early days, as first honorary agent then friend and colleague of George Edwards—"one of the finest men it has ever been my lot to know"—and reflected on the changes wrought in the countryside since 1928: "When I look back over the quarter of a century, and when I reflect on the condition of the land workers then and compare those conditions with today, I am myself astonished at what rural trade unionism has accomplished."

These improvements included a national minimum wage and fixed hours, two weeks' paid holidays and six bank holidays with pay—formerly there was just the odd bank holiday and no other annual vacation at all.

"I think it is true to say that no single class in the country has made so much economic and social progress as the agricultural worker and his family in the last 25 years. There was a time when the landsman, for all his skill which might be grudgingly admitted, was not highly regarded by many, and was generally considered not on a par with the industrial worker. When a farm worker visited the town he could often be easily distinguished. The farm worker of today is not a bit like his grandfather, or even his father. When the delegates come to Cheltenham, which has a reputation for gentility, it will not be possible to pick them out by their clothes, gait, speech or form of behaviour. The wider contacts made possible by the experiences of the war, the development of transport, the movies, the wireless, the spread of popular education—all these have helped to create a new spirit in the countryman. He lives in a larger world. He now takes his place in social and public life, and in the councils of the industry. He attends technical classes and wins scholarships... He has achieved an altogether higher status.

It is gratifying that this progress has been made without resort to stoppages of work. Peaceful negotiations on wages can be made through the Agricultural Wages Board. Any other differences which arise are settled between the workers' and employers' representatives through methods which have been established and developed by mutual consent to afford a medium for both parties to solve questions which inevitably arise."

The Union had greatly expanded its membership, branches and funds. But British agriculture was now the most highly mechanised in the world and "in the future no farmer or farm worker will be able to hold his own without an adequate knowledge of modern farming practice". It was the Agriculture Act and the Agricultural Wages (Regulation) Act brought in by the Labour Government that had put the industry on a sound economic footing.

A few months after these celebrations it was back to urgent matters of the day as the Union marched through London to claim a £7 weekly wage—a rise of one pound—and Edwin addressed the crowd at Speakers' Corner. Farmworkers' wives from Kent led the parade, with placards declaring: "Our members grow the nation a square meal—help them to get a square deal", "Gone with the wind— the purchasing power of the farm workers' pay packet", and "Jam on it? Not if the old man is on the agricultural minimum wage!"

With the power of the unions' block votes firmly behind him, "Ted" Gooch became—from 1946—a permanent fixture of Labour's National Executive Committee, and in 1959 he topped the NEC poll with a whopping 5,321,000 votes.

An election address from 1955 reads: "1945 GOOCH 1950 GOOCH 1951 GOOCH 1955? Well, why not? To ensure continuity of service by a Norfolk man in the interests of the Norfolk people, without regard to party, class or creed. Again Vote GOOCH." (p.86). An additional note echoes the old anxieties of the agricultural worker: "No one need know how you vote but yourself!". Edwin Gooch was one of the few Labour MPs to increase their majority in 1955.

Perhaps partly as a result of this he was elected Chairman of the Labour Party for 1955/6. The *Eastern Daily Press* wished him well: "The honour his party has done him was not, however, due to him for his seniority alone, but for his political sagacity, shrewdness and moderation. The post-war policy of agricultural expansion and rural reform owes much to his guidance behind the scenes, and his opponents respect him as a critic hardly less than his own party values him for advice."

A press photo shows the Chairman in a line of fellow-MPs linking arms on Filey seafront at a 1955 national rally held in Butlin's holiday camp; with Edwin are, amongst others, Barbara Castle, Tom Driberg and Ian Mikardo. He was

MPs IN HOLIDAY MOOD before the start of the Labour Party's national rally now being held at Butlin's camp, Filey. Left to right: Mr Tom Driberg, Mrs Barbara Castle, Mr Edwin Gooch, Miss Alice Bacon, Mr Ian Mikardo, Miss Margaret Herbison, Mr Morgan Phillips (party secretary), Mrs Eirene White, and Mr Wilfred Burke.

also photographed with the retiring party leader Clement Attlee at the Durham Miners' Gala, waving from the balcony of the County Hotel as the massed ranks of coalminers marched past with their banners. Another photo shows Edwin Gooch having a quiet word with Attlee at the press conference in December 1955 at which Clem announced he was stepping down after the General Election defeat. Seen together they seem rather similar, a pair of thoughtful and considerate individuals, quiet but determined. Attlee has his political pipe in hand; Edwin no doubt has his within reach, too, ready for a ruminative smoke.

Looking back almost fifty years, the former Prime Minister Jim Callaghan— elevated to Lord Callaghan of Cardiff—wrote to Simon Gooch in 2003 in response to a query, with an affectionate memoir of Edwin: "In meetings, Ted was always a calm influence, he spoke only when necessary, and then only quietly. I certainly never heard him raise his voice. He was always listened to particularly carefully because of the agricultural connection, which was so weak in the Labour Party in those days".

Edwin's chairmanship of the Labour Party coincided with the Union's Golden Jubilee: "It is not a bad idea to have a countryman as leader of what is mainly a great industrial political party", he declared in an editorial in the *Land Worker*, which came out in a gold cover in both May and June 1956. "What a long way we've come, and how wonderful our advance! I regard our Union as one of the miracles of the Trade Union world... This Union is, above all, a brotherhood."

Edwin Gooch, Chairman of the Labour Party, on the balcony of the County Hotel with the Gaitskells and the Attlees, Durham Miners Gala 1955.

Edwin Gooch, Chairman of the Labour Party, and Clem Attlee at the news conference announcing he will step down as Leader, 1955.

Dinner with Mr Khrushchev

AS luck would have it 1956 was the year in which the USSR's Communist Party General Secretary Nikita Khrushchev and Premier Nikolai Bulganin visited Britain. This was very much a novelty; Stalin had stayed well away from the democratic world. A new wind seemed to be blowing through the Soviet Union, though much remained behind closed doors: Khrushchev made his famous speech denouncing Stalin in February, but its content remained secret.

As part of their UK itinerary in April 1956 the Soviet leaders attended a private dinner, as the guests of Labour's National Executive Committee, that has since become something of a cautionary tale of how not to be diplomatic. Edwin Gooch, as Chairman of the Labour Party and "chair" on the night (and only recently recovered from an emergency operation) made a short speech of welcome to which Bulganin replied. Callaghan then called on Khrushchev to speak. The result was an hour-long harangue against the capitalist West. Richard Crossman wrote in his diary that Khrushchev was "a boss and a bully" who had threatened that if Britain did not join with the Russians "they would swat us off the face of the Earth like a dirty old black beetle".

A bouquet for Karl Marx from visiting Soviet leaders Bulganin and Khrushchev, Highgate 1956.

George Brown MP, fortified by drink, toasted Khrushchev teasingly as a "big boss". Khrushchev replied that Brown looked to him like a little boss. This developed into running banter between the two (and presumably a flustered translator) after the meal as the whisky flowed. As the press later commented, these two bullish individuals had "locked horns".

At one stage in his peroration Khrushchev defended the Molotov-Ribbentrop Pact of 1939, at which George Brown muttered "May God forgive you". Khrushchev demanded to know what he had said and Brown repeated it out loud, at which point "pandemonium" broke out.

Once Khrushchev had ended his diatribe, Labour's new leader, Hugh Gaitskell, made a conciliatory reply, but felt "honour bound" to bring up the subject of imprisoned Social Democrats in Eastern Europe. This seems ill-judged: at a first meeting at the Soviet Embassy the day before, the subject had caused a row. Now it made Khrushchev even angrier. He raged "If you want to help the enemies of the working class, you must find another agent to do it". Nye Bevan wanted to know who were the enemies of the working class and how was their guilt established. The press reported that he wagged a finger at the Russian leader. At this point Khrushchev and entourage stormed out of this "wasted evening".

Edwin Gooch was criticised by Gaitskell (though only privately, in the pages of his diary) for letting things get out of hand; but with two such hotheads as Khrushchev and Brown in close proximity, other Labour grandees—none of whom were shrinking violets—weighing in, and with copious supplies of alcohol available, it seems unfair and peevish to blame him alone for the spat.

A visit by Chairman and Leader to the Russians' suite at Claridges Hotel calmed the situation, and Edwin Gooch features in a Pathé newsreel entering the lobby with Gaitskell. Khrushchev and Hugh Gaitskell shook hands at the House of Commons the next day, but Brown was snubbed. Lord Callaghan recalled in his 2003 letter that "...your grandfather was seated in the centre of the top tables, but I don't think he was able to say much in what you call the crossfire between Khrushchev and George Brown".

In retrospect, however excruciating an experience it must have been for Edwin and many others present, there is something heroically anarchic about this Cold War head-to-head. It was free of hypocrisy, an unbuttoned assertion of both democratic values and absolutist strength. One would imagine that Khrushchev—as Soviet leader—can never have been spoken to like that before. *Time* magazine, in its report, called it "The Night of the Long Spoons".

Gaitskell-Gooch relations may have been further strained (though Edwin was in many ways a natural supporter of that centrist politician) when the party leader attended the National Union of Agricultural Workers' Golden Jubilee Biennial parade at Great Yarmouth in June 1956. He was photographed marching along the seafront before a Union banner with Edwin Gooch, Harold Collison and others. But then, in the lounge of the Star Hotel, came Gaitskell's fateful encounter with Edwin's grandson Simon, then a one-year-old extremist, who—like a miniature Khrushchev—smashed a tiny fist against the guest of honour's cup and saucer, spilling tea all over the Labour Party's 'lost leader'.

Nevertheless, Gaitskell's speech at the Marina was a cheerful one: "He, the President and General Secretary, had all marched in step from the beginning to

Labour leader Hugh Gaitskell, flanked by Edwin Gooch, President, and Harold Collison, General Secretary, at the NUAW's Golden Jubilee celebrations in Great Yarmouth, 1956.

the end of the parade and he suggested that there was probably some significance in the fact that the Leader of the Labour Party, the Leader of the Parliamentary Party and a member of the TUC General Council could all be in unison. He pledged to abolish tied cottage evictions when Labour next came to power".

Gaitskell would later come up to North Walsham, in 1961, to open the new North Norfolk Labour Party constituency office, Edwin House. All was forgotten and forgiven.

Edwin Gooch presided over the Labour Party Conference at Blackpool in 1956 (considered "the best since 1945") at which the Suez Crisis took centre stage, with an emergency resolution denouncing the Eden Government's "lamentable handling" of the affair. At the conclusion of events Edwin received this vote of thanks from the NEC: "He has guided the Conference with a quiet confidence—but this is what we expect of a man with his feet so firmly planted on good soil". He wound up proceedings with a Presidential Address: "Our resolve must be to work for the common good; to feed, clothe and shelter the depressed and the helpless; and not to spare ourselves until nation is drawn unto nation in peace and goodwill".

Smaller-scale political gatherings are recorded in various press photographs. In several of them Nye Bevan addresses a Union rally against the tied cottage, in about 1959. Bevan had criticised the NUAW and other unions' moderate leaderships in a *Tribune* pamphlet in 1951, but continued to speak at farmworkers' events.

In 1954 Edwin Gooch had been widely acclaimed for speaking out against German rearmament, but "this did not make him a Bevanite" - i.e. a unilateral disarmer (if pushed he might have described himself politically as a "Morrisonite"). But then at the 1957 Labour Party Conference he supported Bevan's switch to a multilateral position, which Nye marked with his famous phrase condemning unilateralism as sending any British foreign minister "naked into the council chamber". However, nuclear tests should be unilaterally brought to an end, said Bevan, to give the United Kingdom the moral advantage.

Nye Bevan speaks at an NUAW rally against the tied cottage. Edwin Gooch, cigarette in mouth, ruminates.

In 1958 Edwin wrote about the madness of the arms race, "Better to talk to those from other lands about freeing the world from want of food...", and in 1960, perhaps inspired by the rise of the Campaign for Nuclear Disarmament, he joined Labour Party Conference delegates in voting in favour of getting rid of nuclear weapons. This was the occasion of Gaitskell's famous "Fight and fight again" speech against the motion, which he lost but then reversed in 1961. In 1962 Edwin wrote "We live in a disturbing age... World disarmament must be the goal".

He underwent another operation in the summer of 1958, but recovered quickly and was straight off to the International Labour Organisation in Geneva, and a few months later in Copenhagen he was re-elected President of the International Landworkers' Federation. At the Party Conference in Scarborough that year Edwin Gooch introduced Labour's document on agricultural policy, *Prosper the Plough*, subtitled "a policy for a sound and efficient British agriculture", which proposed, as Edwin said, "moderate expansion... This may not be exciting either to the Conference, or the farming community, but it is immeasurably reassuring compared with the standstill policy of the present Tory Government".

Edwin Gooch, Labour NEC, on the conference platform in Scarborough, 1960, when Hugh Gaitskell gave his famous speech against unilateral disarmament. Harold Wilson looks on.

In February 1959 the *Land Worker* wished the President a happy 70th birthday: "A man who has worked in the interests of agricultural workers for most of his life, he is still able to put vigour, backed by a wealth of experience, into all he does. In fact, during the period surrounding his birthday he made two trips abroad in the interests of international trade unionism and solidarity.

Bro.Gooch has been the Union's president for the past thirty years. He brings to the council chamber some of the hard-headed common sense for which his home county of Norfolk is famous. May he continue to do so for many years to come!"

E.G.Gooch won North Norfolk again in the 1959 General Election, with a majority of 658.

Caricature of Edwin Gooch from the Land Worker, 1959.

An East Anglian First and Foremost

IN 1960 Edwin George Gooch married Mary Agatha "Mollie" Curl, whom he had got to know over the years when sitting with fellow-councillors and journalists at his regular table at Woolworth's cafeteria in Norwich (which had housed a big Union celebration in 1937, with Hugh Dalton and Ben Tillett as guests). At Woolies, Mollie was famed for her artistically iced cakes. She was a Norwich girl, born in 1911, the daughter of a licensed victualler and one of three highly communicative sisters. Mollie had a son, David Curl, to whom she was devoted.

Edwin Gooch married Mollie Curl in 1960.

Mollie was a long-time Labour supporter and activist. Though she was a Roman Catholic and Edwin a Methodist that was no object to their marriage in Norwich's mighty Roman Catholic church (now cathedral) of St John the Baptist, with Michael as his father's best man. A photograph in the *Eastern Daily*

Press showed the couple cutting the cake at the Royal Hotel. They were off on honeymoon "in the Shakespeare country".

Much earlier, in 1952, Edwin had participated in an Audience with Pope Pius XII at Castel Gandolfo, during a United Nations Food and Agriculture Organisation Conference in Rome, its permanent home. He was slightly defensive in the *Land Worker's* subsequent report: "In

Wedding reception for Edwin and Mollie Gooch, Royal Hotel, Norwich, 1960.

accepting the invitation of the Pope there was no religious significance... I am not a Catholic but a Methodist by conviction. But I believe in religious freedom and I regarded it as a privilege... I was presented as a Member of the British Parliament. The Pope shook me warmly by the hand and gave me a cordial welcome."

As a working MP in his seventies, and increasingly unwell, the indomitable Mollie's support was vital. Her ability to drive was a major asset; until then Edwin had relied on public transport, while for visits to deeper rural areas the NUAW had provided cars, such as an ancient Daimler in Wymondham with a speaking tube connecting to the sealed-off chauffeur.

At the Labour Party Conference in Blackpool in 1961 Edwin Gooch, aged 72, did not seek re-election to the NEC. Entries in his name in *Hansard* come to an end in November that year, but he spoke at the 1962 Labour Party Conference in Brighton against joining the Common Market. Though his health was never good again he stayed active in many areas: as well as Westminster and his constituency, he remained President of the NUAW and a prominent figure in international trade unionism. In Norfolk he was still a JP, Alderman, Vice-Chairman of Norfolk County Council and Chair of its Education and Agricultural Education Committees.

Should he have retired altogether from public life at this point? Perhaps so, though his strong sense of duty would no doubt have prevented him. Edwin Gooch MP's entry in *Who's Who* for 1962 includes a telling detail: "Recreations—public, social and political work." No golf or stamp-collecting for him. Undoubtedly Mollie's energy and enthusiasm kept him going in these later years. He outlived Hugh Gaitskell, who died in his fifties in January 1963 and was succeeded as Labour leader by Harold Wilson.

Though Edwin was a forward-looking man, it is difficult to imagine him among the younger generation of Labour politicians who came to prominence in the Sixties. He probably seemed a figure from another era to them—Tam Dalyell, writing an obituary for the NUAAW's great left-wing campaigner Joan Maynard MP in 1998, described Edwin Gooch, in his rather lofty manner, as "sedate". Perhaps he was in some ways, though he had perseverance and dedication to match his younger colleague. And when Dalyell first entered Parliament in 1962 Edwin was not a well man.

For now Edwin Gooch carried on, his commitment to the socialist cause pretty much unstoppable, and still with telling effect. In October 1963 *Land Worker* announced that the Union had won a minimum wage of £9-10/- for a 45 hour week. In the last piece he wrote for the journal, a New Year Message for 1964, Edwin claimed "The day of the skilled technician has arrived".

A series of professional photos from the turn of the Sixties show a patriarchal Edwin Gooch signing autographs and hosting groups of Norfolk schoolchildren and lady constituents (all in their Sunday best) on the sunny terrace of the House of Commons.

Around this time Edwin was a guest on a BBC Home Service programme, *That Reminds Me*, on which he confirmed his real loyalties: "My roots lie in East Anglia, and what I was taught and learned in Norfolk has governed my outlook in life. I am an East Anglian first and foremost". The *Radio Times* profiled him under the sub-head *Farm-worker's Friend*: "It is highly improbable that any living man has done more to further the interest of the farm-worker in this country than Alderman E.G.Gooch... Not only is he greatly loved by his members; he has also earned the respect and admiration of farmers everywhere... He is an international figure in his own field, having held a number of high offices in world organisations, and I suppose this tough but quietly spoken man is as well known

abroad as he is at home." Anglia Television profiled Edwin Gooch on his 75th birthday in January 1964: "They asked me to say what I liked and I did".

In his Presidential Address to the June 1964 National Union of Agricultural Workers' Biennial Conference at Felixstowe (at which he was unanimously re-elected President), Edwin—by then in very poor health and with Vice-President

Edwin Gooch flanked by Albert Hilton MP and Harold Collison, General Secretary, NUAW Biennial.

Edwin Gooch [North Norfolk] and Albert Hilton [South-West Norfolk] celebrate their election victories in 1959. Edwin's agent Arthur Amis, standing at left.

Albert Hilton acting as Chairman for much of the business—had been as combative as ever, criticising farmers for resisting legitimate wage rises.

In "a moving passage" he was optimistic about the next Government:

"When Labour is elected—and I am confident that NUAW members and the public at large will see to it that Labour is in office after the coming Election—I shall be watching from the wings. But I shall be watching content in the knowledge that the agricultural industry is to be run along lines which the Union has helped to fashion.

We are very definite on one thing—there will always be a need for a separate Union for the agricultural and allied workers".

The new Head Office (designed by his architect son Michael) would be built by the time of the next Biennial, replacing the old Headland House that had seen the Union grow into a force to be reckoned with in the countryside.

"There will be plenty of room for expansion within the fine new building that is now going up. Our task must be to see that expansion takes place. Expansion not only in size, but in effectiveness, in influence, in prestige—and in results. I am confident that with a proper contribution from all—and I use that word to cover all its meanings—we shall be equal to the task. And so long as we are, the

Edwin and Mollie entertain the family at Rydal Mount c1960, including his future biographer.

future well-being of the farm and rural workers need never be in doubt."

He was making an heroic effort to keep going, but eventually he had to concede defeat. I have a sad and strange memory of being taken to *Rydal Mount* one hot summer's day and finding Grandpa lying on a bed downstairs in the sitting room. It was all very puzzling for a small boy. On 2nd August 1964, just a few months before the autumn General Election (for which he had already stood down in favour of his old Wymondham comrade, Bert Hazell), Edwin died at home.

His last public appearance had been at the Mulbarton Church Parade, where he presented a long-serving NUAW member, Bro. Andrews, with a silver badge. As a tribute to Edwin in the September *Land Worker* made clear "He was never happier than when he was with the rank and file and particularly if he was in Norfolk—the county which he loved and served so well".

LAND WORKER

JOURNAL OF THE NATIONAL UNION OF AGRICULTURAL WORKERS

SEPTEMBER 1964
PRICE TWOPENCE

Union members everywhere mourn the death of their President Edwin Gooch

Front cover of Land Worker, September 1964, mourning President Edwin Gooch.

Champion of the Farmworkers

BERT Hazell held North Norfolk on 15th October 1964 by just 53 votes, but Labour had—as Edwin predicted—won at last, and Harold Wilson had a small working majority in the Commons.

Bert had earlier paid personal tribute to his predecessor in the pages of the *Eastern Daily Press*:

"My association with Edwin Gooch goes back to my teenage days when I worked on a farm at Wymondham and joined the NUAW and he used to cycle to the villages round Wymondham on behalf of the union.

"Wherever Edwin Gooch went... he always proclaimed the virtues of the county in which he was born and lived. There is no denying that he was a great champion of Norfolk, its traditions and its people. The county has suffered a great loss in his passing."

Hazell had met Edwin shortly before he died; laconic as ever, his last words to him had been a simple "Cheerio, Bert".

Edwin Gooch: "I am a countryman at heart".

It was particularly appropriate that the *Norwich Mercury* should pay a strong tribute, hailing "a most distinguished son of Norfolk":

"Edwin Gooch goes into history as a stalwart of the Labour Party, which he had served for a year as its national chairman; as a notable and highly effective figure in trade unionism, being widely known in Europe as well as among his fellow countrymen; and as a man whose breadth of vision in agricultural matters greatly transcended the merely partisan or political principles which might otherwise have hopelessly estranged the representatives of the workers and the employers. There is no doubt that the personal influence of Mr Gooch—often in negotiations which have been hard and long—has been very much to do with the establishment in agriculture of working relations which are the envy of many other industries.

'E.G.G.' (the initials were much more familiar publicly than his Christian name, Edwin) is especially remembered this week by older members of the 'Norwich Mercury' Series, for it was on these papers, in 1911, that he started what was to be the whole of his career in full-time journalism...

Right to the last, however, he was eagerly interested in the newspapers which he himself had served for so long, and the present Editor of the 'Norwich Mercury' Series, who is grateful for having enjoyed Edwin Gooch's friendship for some 20 years, was in conversation with him only a fortnight before he died. The meeting took place on the Royal Norfolk Showground, at Costessey, and the occasion was the county rally of the Norfolk and Norwich Federation of Young Farmers' Clubs. It was an uncomfortably hot day, yet Edwin Gooch, although weak from illness, found pleasure in having been driven there by his wife; it was the sort of event he never liked to miss. Of such stuff was 'E.G.G.' made; doughty, determined and faithful."

The obituary in the *Times* for Alderman Edwin Gooch was headlined 'STURDY CHAMPION OF FARMWORKERS':

"Edwin Gooch's long career in trade unionism and the organization of the Labour Party was solid rather than spectacular. He was generally regarded as a moderate and a man of the centre rather than the left. But he lived to see his organization achieving much more success than might have been prophesied when he joined it. His union policy consolidated the gains in status which had to be given the farmworker as a result of war exigencies and postwar developments; cooperation rather than competition with other agricultural interests gave his members an improving share in the fruits of government support to British farming. At the same time the organization became influential in trade union policies to an extent far beyond what might have been inferred from its status and membership when he first became involved with it.

A rare photograph of the President of the NUAW setting foot on a farm.

His thinking, like his speech, betrayed a typical East Anglian background of unexcited radical nonconformity, firm in its convictions and determined in their pursuit—the same stock and tradition from which the backbone of the Cromwellian army came. To the end of his life he devoted as much time and energy to the affairs of his native Norfolk as he did to those beyond it. It was significant that those of his acquaintance who did not address him by his Christian name usually called him Alderman. That was an office in which he was always happy."

Land Worker devoted five pages of its September 1964 issue to a tribute to the late President; the cover headlined "Union members everywhere mourn the death of their President Edwin Gooch". His passing "extinguished a torch that has shone at the head of our Union for thirty-four years". The eulogies began with an editorial, *End of an Era*:

"Bro. Edwin Gooch, President of our Union for the past 34 years, died on August 2nd at his home in Wymondham, Norfolk. He was 75 years of age. His passing is felt as a personal loss to all of us in the Union, but he is also mourned much further afield—in individual country homes, in the wider trades union and Labour movement, in local and national government circles and at international level.

"In the history of our Union the name of Edwin Gooch will always be writ large and bold, and to many it might seem that his death marks the end of a chapter. In fact it marks the end of an era. For Edwin was the last of a few public spirited men who, although never farm workers themselves, came to the assistance of those who in the early days struggled to get the Union on its feet. They gave of their spare time, their knowledge and their ability, and took advantage of their relative independence, to build up the Union into an effective organisation.

Their talents and their energies were welcomed by the members; and it is not surprising that some, Edwin among them, were elected to important offices. But his role outstayed them all. While he watched and worked, the Union grew. His influence has left an indelible mark on its outlook, its activities and its policies.

In our sadness we can also take pride, as he did, that under his leadership the NUAW grew not only in size but in effectiveness, in influence and prestige. And with it the status of rural workers throughout the country.

Edwin was a fighter of Norfolk stock. He was born, lived and died in a town that four hundred years ago was the centre of a famous revolt against the injustices of the times. Kett's rebellion was a bloody affair. Edwin was a peaceable man; but his life's work against the injustices of his times was certainly more effective than that of his famous predecessor. And the best way we can honour his memory is to start the new era by carrying on that fight from where he had to leave off."

Letters of condolence had come in to head office from far and wide, including from I.Shkuratov, President of the USSR Agricultural Workers' Union. Mukdim Osmay of the International Labour Organisation wrote: "His long Presidentship of the ILF served to promote an awareness of the urgent need everywhere to do more for those making their living from the land". Sir John Winnifrith, Permanent Secretary of the Ministry of Agriculture, Fisheries and Food, wrote: "He always seemed to me to personify the rugged fighting qualities for which East Anglia has always been famous".

Tributes came in from the branches. From Norfolk: "I served under him on the Wages Committee when the meetings were not friendly affairs, but Edwin Gooch always kept cool, calm and collected—he was really a great leader at all times".

And from (theoretical) opponents such as Christopher Soames MP, Minister of Agriculture: "Although we were on opposite sides of the political fence, his complete sincerity and deep concern for the interests of all who derive their living from the land were universally respected". Sir Harold Woolley, the National Farmers Union President, hailed Edwin Gooch as "a realist who saw clearly that the interests of the members of his Union were inextricably linked with the prosperity of the whole industry. In his many public duties he was dedicated and unsparing in his efforts. As a friend and colleague his personality reflected the basic qualities of sincerity, kindliness and common sense. Agriculture has lost a pillar of strength".

NUAW General Secretary Harold Collison wrote the chief Tribute:

"The passing of Edwin Gooch at the beginning of last month extinguished a torch that has shone at the head of our Union for the past thirty-four years. His work was at an end; but the Union to which he gave so much and which owes so much to him goes on—a living tribute to his life and work.

Edwin had exceeded man's allotted span by five years, but he was active in his work till only a short time before his death. Few crammed so much into their lives as he did and his activities provide an astonishing chronicle of service; service to his county, to his country, to his Union and to his Party. Service, in fact, to his fellow-men.

In his first decade as President "it was slow, hard uphill work" for the Union until the outbreak of hostilities in 1939. "Throughout this time he campaigned up and down the country and in his native Norfolk for the cause of the farm worker and farming. And in this work he was among the early few who swam against the tide of the times in calling for Government support and protection for agriculture. With the coming of the war this became automatic, but there can be no doubt that the influence of Edwin Gooch and a few others with similar views went a long way to establishing the school of thought which resulted in the passing of Labour's renowned Agriculture Act in 1947.

It has been my privilege to be the fifth of the Union's General Secretaries to have the experience of working with Edwin Gooch. The association was both close and harmonious and one was always conscious of the fact that one was working with a man whose contribution to the work of the movement would earn him a place in history alongside such revered figures as those of Joseph Arch and George Edwards. His personal character and qualities were so patent that it was easy to understand the very real affection with which he was held by all who knew him."

Mrs Gooch's supportive role was acknowledged by Harold Collison:

"It has also been a joy to see the very great happiness which came from the union with his second wife—Mollie, as she is known to us all. A man who was lonely became complete again. A house that seemed empty became a home again. A wonderful partnership developed which brought happiness to them both, and it has been Mollie's care and devotion these last few years which has enabled Edwin to carry out much work which he might have otherwise not been able to undertake."

The journal revealed more of his stoicism: "For most of his life Edwin Gooch enjoyed excellent health. His first setback came in 1956 when he was suddenly taken ill... He quickly recovered but in 1958 underwent another operation and for the first time since he became President he was unable to attend the Biennial Conference of that year.

"Subsequently most people would have thought that he had returned to full health, but in fact he often suffered considerable pain... No-one except those nearest to him heard him complain, and they only very infrequently. But last Christmas he had another setback—one from which he never really recovered. He must have drawn on tremendous reserves of willpower to attend this year's Biennial Conference at Felixstowe. But in the weeks that followed his illness forced him to seek excusal from most of his public work. Yet when the General Secretary saw him at his home a day or two before he died he still wanted to do all he could for himself."

Looking back over this period Harold Collison, in a public tribute, mourned "a man of the highest possible integrity... He was one of the most courageous men I have ever known."

As reported in the *Eastern Daily Press*, another old colleague, Albert Hilton MP, said that Norfolk had lost one of its leading public figures, the British farm workers their greatest champion and the Labour Party a most loyal member:

"For many years he was the leader of the workers' side of the Norfolk Agricultural Wages Board and was almost hated by Norfolk farmers. But by his sincerity and integrity he had become in recent years accepted and respected by the whole of the farming community, and a few years ago he was elected president of the Royal Norfolk Agricultural Association, the only workers' representative to receive such an honour.

He was never content with being just a member of a committee or a body, but played a full part in everything he was interested in.

Edwin Gooch was a friendly man with friends in all walks of life. He was often the guest of leading people in the country and although he enjoyed these occasions, he was always happiest in the company of ordinary members of the NUAW, the people in whose service he lived and who now mourn the loss of their leader."

The *Eastern Daily Press* added other tributes. George Woodcock, General Secretary of the TUC described him as "a grand old man". Conservative MPs from the region joined in the tributes, notably John Hill, member for South Norfolk and his 'pair' in the Commons: "I am terribly sorry to hear of his death. Edwin will be greatly missed. He was a distinguished leader in the agricultural world and although we were on different sides we were great friends. He took on a tremendous burden of public work and would never let up on his services to the County Council, Parliament or NUAW."

Other press comment was quoted in *Land Worker*. The *Eastern Daily Press*: "It was his forthright honesty in what he stood for which won him honour nationally and in the trade union movement, and recognition internationally in agricultural affairs". The *East Anglian Daily Times*: "Edwin Gooch was a product of a hard school and held on to his beliefs with such sincerity that he was often the centre of controversy. The fact that he always conducted controversy with courtesy did not lessen his determination nor weaken his opinions. Among these was an inherent disapproval of things as they used to be in rural areas."

The funeral service at Wymondham Methodist Church was covered in some detail in the September *Land Worker*, under the headline "The Last Journey". The cortège had wound through the town, preceded by Fred Mayhew carrying the banner of the Wymondham & Silfield branch of the NUAW. Numerous Union officials were present, as well as Edwin's old friend Adrian de Ruyter, General Secretary of the European Landworkers' Federation, who had flown over from Holland to pay his last respects.

Lord Wise had spoken: "When the history of Norfolk men and women of this century comes to be written, there will be many references to Edwin Gooch and his name will be remembered and revered… He was a quiet man with nothing flamboyant or self-seeking about him, his every endeavour aimed at doing what would be helpful to those in need."

The service ended with a minute's silence, followed by a benediction from the Bishop of Norwich, Dr Lancelot Fleming.

Edwin's great-niece Pat Salmon remembered the day: "I went to Uncle Ted's funeral, terribly moving, all those agricultural workers in collars and ties. The chapel was full, all denominations of clergy there. We progressed through the town, his Union banner carried before him. People stood in doorways, hats were doffed, as we went to the cemetery. I cried!"

At a Memorial Service at Wymondham Abbey, on 13th September 1964, "a sad, yet sunny occasion", a great congregation "crammed into the sunlit Abbey as Mrs Mollie Gooch and members of Edwin's family walked down the aisle". Edwin Gooch was described by the Chairman of the County Council as "a great son of Norfolk". His long-standing agent in North Norfolk, Arthur Amis, spoke of a gallant and courageous man who had carved for himself a niche in the history of Norfolk… He knew how to give and not count the cost, and his philosophy was bound to the Christian principle of making the world a better place for his fellow men. Albert Hilton MP said that farmworkers regarded him as their champion, and that Edwin's memorial was already in every village in the land—the new look achieved for farmworkers in his lifetime.

At both funeral and memorial, the congregation sang the old Methodist hymn:

These things shall be: a loftier race
Than e'er the world hath known shall rise,
With flame of freedom in their souls
And light of knowledge in their eyes

Present at my grandfather's Memorial Service as a boy, I remember a forest of black trouser legs and a low rumble of Norfolk-accented conversation in the shadow of the great church on a hot summer's day, then the sound of hymns sung heartily coming through the open door while I, my sister and young cousins, played uncomprehendingly among the gravestones and the pines.

In the October 1964 issue of *Land Worker* there was 'A Final Tribute' from 93-year-old Herbert Harvey of Trunch, the last surviving pioneer from the Union's 1906 inaugural meeting:

"Believe me, the loss of Edwin Gooch caused my old heart to ache. I felt I could not face the funeral; you see he was my best friend. At a Conference of the Union in 1928 George Edwards proposed Edwin Gooch should be President... I had earlier noticed a young fellow taking down shorthand and took him for a press reporter (which he was) sitting with Tom Higdon. I asked about him—not having met him previously. It was Edwin Gooch.

When he got into the chair and began to talk about a new policy for the Union I was thrilled by his speech. We had got a winner. My first actual contact with him was on the Agricultural Wages Committee for Norfolk. He put up his case for a raise in wages; he impressed me more than any man I'd met. A leader of men, I thought. So he proved..."

Soon after his death an Edwin Gooch Appeal began to raise funds towards a bursary to educate each year a young man or woman in agriculture.

Mollie stayed on at *Rydal Mount* for some years, then moved back to Norwich to live near her larger-than-life sister Nelly. The Wymondham house was let, part of the garden built over, and finally it was sold. The sisters' houses in George Borrow Road on the Earlham estate were situated more-or-less back to back, and these two increasingly rotund figures were constantly to-ing and fro-ing. They were a joy to visit down the years, a very 'Norwich' double act, full of good cheer and strong opinions. Mollie lived for more than thirty years after Edwin died; hyper-active to the last she was still doing good works in her no-nonsense and indefatigable way, ferrying frail members of the congregation of St John's around,

A late portrait of Edwin Gooch MP, taken at Brighton.

and of course baking and icing cakes galore. The Roman Catholic Cathedral was full for her funeral in 1997, as a soprano sang *Ave Maria*.

Years later, Edwin's successor as NUAW President and North Norfolk MP, Bert Hazell, gave a frank but sympathetic judgement on Edwin's role in the Union when I visited him in his office at the London headquarters on Gray's Inn Road: "Edwin and Ethel were both hard workers. He was a very good President, but he had his limitations. I don't think he really understood the farmworker, he trained as a journalist and found it difficult to get down to their level. He made tremendous sacrifices for the Union. I often think of him when an old man, waiting on some lonely railway platform on a cold night after addressing a meeting. He was sometimes taken in by the farmers into believing that they couldn't afford any more than they offered. He was never aggressive enough from the farmworkers' point of view. He was too kindly".

Maybe so, but he achieved much through his patient negotiations and could write and speak stirringly in public on the farmworkers' behalf, and *Hansard* testifies to his unflagging promotion of their cause. It was a matter of deep, unwavering faith. In 1938 he addressed the NUAW's Biennial Conference, describing their movement as a "real mighty, moving spiritual force which can carry all before it".

*The ploughteam symbol of the NUAW, adapted for the
National Union of Agricultural & Allied Workers, continued
to be used by the Rural, Agricultural & Allied Workers section
of first the T&GWU, then Unite.*

Unite

THE new offices for the National Union of Agricultural Workers at 308 Gray's Inn Road, London, designed by Michael Gooch and retaining the name *Headland House*, were opened in 1966 by George Woodcock, General Secretary of the TUC. The building contained an Edwin Gooch Memorial Library. Appropriately enough, in the light of Edwin's dual role in trade unionism, the National Union of Journalists bought the site next door and built an almost matching block as their headquarters.

But was this another advance for the Union, or a memorial in concrete and steel to its great days gone by?

From the mid-Sixties mechanisation meant that the rural workforce was much reduced, even on big Norfolk farms. The old rural world was disappearing, as I witnessed for myself from the end of the decade when my parents bought an old farmhouse near the Waveney Valley. We had the house and garden of what had been a hundred acre farm, a size which was no longer sustainable; its modest fields had been absorbed by a much larger neighbour, with wholesale loss of trees and hedges. An old waggon sat unused in the barn, along with horse collars from which straw was bursting; the copper and the bread oven became purely decorative features.

The Old Boys were disappearing, too. But for those who remained on the farms the relationship between 'master and man', perhaps as a result of reduced numbers, became more relaxed and companionable, without its old formality and tendency towards authoritarianism; the tied cottage finally went, thanks to the Rent (Agricultural) Act passed in 1976, but wages remained low and insecure.

As a result of this steady erosion of its strength, confidence and resources, the National Union of Agricultural and Allied Workers—as it was renamed in 1968, to acknowledge forestry workers and food factory staff—voted (after much emotional debate) to merge with the giant Transport & General Workers Union in 1982. The NUAAW became its Agricultural and Allied National Trade Group, and now the Rural, Agricultural and Allied Workers Trade Group within the renamed Unite. Even Wilf Page, the only Communist member of the Executive Committee, regretted the change; in retrospect, he thought, "that old Methodist, democratic approach" could have sustained an independent farm workers' union. The last NUAAW General Secretary, Jack Boddy, seems to have decided that the failing finances of the union left them no option.

Ironically, the merger echoed a proposal by Edwin Gooch at the Biennial Conference in 1924 when he had urged amalgamation with the Workers' Union, an affiliate of the T&GWU. A similar proposal in 1939 had been shelved during the war and made irrelevant by the great boost in NUAW numbers in the Forties. That, however, was to prove the peak of the Union's strength.

The NUAAW head office was vacated after amalgamation and the NUJ moved across from their building next door. The 1966 commemorative plaque from *Headland House* is now mounted on one of the TUC's Martyrs Cottages at Tolpuddle.

Until the 1982 merger, there had been an annual Memorial Service at Edwin and Ethel's grave in Wymondham Cemetery, organised by the NUAAW. In 1978, the 14th such event was reported in the *Eastern Daily Press*. Edwin Gooch's two agents spoke: Mr Arthur Amis had conducted the service; Mr Wilf Page recalled Edwin as an international figure in the trade union movement. Mollie Gooch was present.

In 1989 a new office for the North Norfolk Labour Party was opened in Mount Street, Cromer, by Roy Hattersley MP, Deputy Leader, and named Edwin Gooch House.

Though the old Union has gone the campaigning and organising goes on, and a proud history is celebrated. *Landworker* is published with considerable style, in full colour, by Unite, and in its pages there is often a discernible nostalgia for the old days of an independent Union. In 2019 the journal celebrated its centenary. Despite the protective shield of Unite, the battle to bring back the Agricultural Wages Board in England, after its abolition by the Coalition Government in 2013, is at the time of writing unresolved.

There is an annual festival at the Burston Strike School, and the traditional TUC parade at Tolpuddle every summer; both, as ever, feature the wonderful old National Union of Agricultural Workers banners and brass bands playing *The Red Flag*. As Edwin Gooch wrote in the *Land Worker* in September 1937: "It is still a great experience to revisit the pretty Dorset village; to gain inspiration on the ground those fine men trod; and to vow again as did George Loveless—'We will, we will, we will be free!'"

Bibliography, Sources and Acknowledgments

EDWIN Gooch's role in the National Union of Agricultural Workers is examined in several books: *Sharpen the Sickle* by Reg Groves, 1949 [Porcupine Press, 1949, and Merlin Books reprint, 1981]; *The Deferential Worker* by Howard Newby [Penguin, 1977]; *Poor Labouring Men* by Alun Howkins [Routledge, 1985]; and *Skilled at All Trades—the history of the farmworkers' union 1947-1984* by Bob Wynn [TGWU/Frontline, 1993]. Edwin Gooch was asked by George Edwards to put his autobiography *From Crow Scaring to Westminster* "into shape", though said that he left it just as it was [Labour Publishing Co Ltd, 1922, and Larks Press reprint 2008]; Noel G Edwards told his father's full story in *Ploughboy's Progress—The Life of Sir George Edwards* [Centre for East Anglian Studies, UEA, 1998]. Edwin Gooch also features in the biography of his agent *Norfolk Red—The Life of Wilf Page, Countryside Communist* by Mike Pentelow [Lawrence & Wishart, 2009]. Susan Wild's biography of her public-spirited grandfather *Sam Peel, A Man Who Did Different* is subtitled "one man's impact on a town and a county", that town being Wells-next-the-Sea [Wells Local History Group, 2013].

Edwin and Ethel Gooch's public roles in Wymondham are detailed in various local histories, including *When War came to Wymondham, 1939-45* by Adrian and Anne Hoare [Poppyland Publishing, 2019].

The NUAW archive is at the Museum of English Rural Life, part of Reading University. A full set of bound volumes of the *Land Worker* up to the 1982 merger were donated to the Modern Records Centre at the University of Warwick by Unite in 2019. The Museum of Norfolk Life, Gressenhall, and the People's History Museum in Manchester have some splendid NUALRW and NUAW banners. Gressenhall also has a local archive of NUAW photos and printed matter. The Labour Party Archive is housed in the People's History Museum.

Special thanks are due to Mike Pentelow, former editor of *Landworker*; Adrian and Anne Hoare and the staff of Wymondham Heritage Museum for mounting displays about Edwin and Ethel that have kept their names alive in their hometown and beyond; and to Sir Norman Lamb, erstwhile Liberal Democrat MP for North Norfolk, for his generosity in opening an exhibition on his predecessor Edwin Gooch MP at the Wymondham Heritage Museum.

Index

Fleming, Dr Lancelot, 117
Food and Agriculture Organisation [FAO], 77-78, 81, 106
Forehoe District Council, 33, 49, 52, 59
Forehoe Union, 47
'From Crow-Scaring to Westminster', 35, 60

Gaitskell, Hugh, 100-103, 106
'Gas House' [Wymondham], 13
Gem Orchestra, 48
General Strike, 37-38, 47, 56
George V, King, 15, 17
George VI, King, 68
German Prisoners of War, 77-78
Gill, Eric, 62
Gladstone, William Ewart, 9, 24
Gooch family
    Albert, 6, 8-9, 23, 28
    Bill, 10-11, 19
    Edwin, 2-13, 15-20, 23-24, 26-30, 33-48, 51-60, 62-64, 66-68, 70-73, 75-82, 84-94, 96-108, 111-119, 121-122
    Elizabeth, 7
    Ellen, 7-8, 10-12, 19, 48 [mother of Edwin Gooch, see Stackard, Ellen]
    Ethel, 8 [sister of Edwin Gooch, and wife of Victor Hayes]
    Ethel, 18, 21, 23, 27-29, 37, 46-49, 53, 64-65,, 71, 89-91, 119, 122 [wife of Edwin Gooch, see Banham, Ethel]
    Frederick, 7-8
    James, 7
    Joanna, 92
    John, 7
    Laura Matilda, 7
    Lilian, 8 [see Reyner, Lily]
    Michael, 8, 18, 20-21, 37, 47, 49, 56, 63, 65, 72, 75, 77-78, 89, 105, 108, 121
    Mollie, 4, 105-106, 109, 115-118, 122 [see Curl, Mary Agatha "Mollie"]
    Sheila, 92 [see Ward, Sheila]
    Simon, 6-12, 19 [father of Edwin Gooch]
    Simon, 92
    William, 7
Good Templar Order / Grand Lodge, 11
Gosling, Harry, 41
Great Hockham Village School, 19
Great Yarmouth, 70, 82, 100-101
Groves, Reg, 29, 56, 64
Gurdon, William, 75

Haggard, H. Rider, 36
Hammett, James, 62
'Hansard', 77, 106
Harvey, Herbert, 118
Harvey, Sarah, 7
Hattersley, Roy, 122
Hayes, Freda, 69 [see Lane, Freda]
Hayes, Kevin, 69
Hayes, Victor, 19
Hazell, Bert, 70, 109, 111-112, 119
Hewitt, George, 24-25, 39, 51, 60, 82
Higdon, Annie, 25, 62, 68
Higdon, Tom, 25-26, 30, 32, 34, 39-40, 46, 51-52, 56, 61-62, 68, 118
Hill, John, 117
Hill Farming Bill [1946], 78
Hilton, Albert, 90, 107-108, 116, 118
Hingham Grammar School, 52-53
Hingham, Labour Rally, 42
Holkham Bay, 21
Holmes, Bill, 25, 46, 51, 56, 64
Homerton College [Cambridge], 19
Housing Act [1924], 43
Housing Bill, 89
Howkins, Professor Alun, 5, 45-46, 53-54
Hubbard, Thomas, 8

You may also like

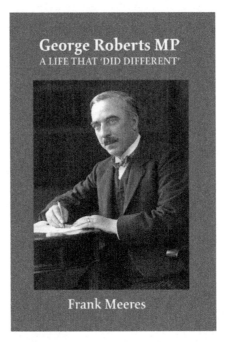

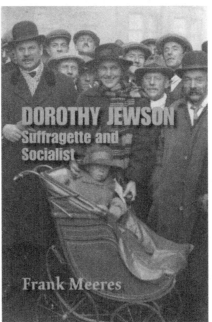

Printed in Great Britain
by Amazon